AAT

AQ2016

Business Tax
(Finance Act 2020)

EXAM KIT

This Exam Kit supports study for the following AAT qualifications:

AAT Professional Diploma in Accounting – Level 4

AAT Level 4 Diploma in Business Skills

AAT Professional Diploma in Accounting at SCQF Level 8

KAPLAN

PUBLISHING

British Library Cataloguing-in-Publication Data

A catalogue record for this book is available from the British Library.

Published by:

Kaplan Publishing UK

Unit 2 The Business Centre

Molly Millar's Lane

Wokingham

Berkshire

RG41 2QZ

ISBN: 978-1-78740-810-4

Acknowledgements

We are grateful to HM Revenue and Customs for the provision of tax forms, which are Crown Copyright and are reproduced here with kind permission from the Office of Public Sector Information.

Kaplan Publishing are constantly finding new ways to make a difference to your studies and our exciting online resources really do offer something different to students looking for exam success.

This book comes with free MyKaplan online resources so that you can study anytime, anywhere. **This free online resource is not sold separately and is included in the price of the book.**

Having purchased this book, you have access to the following online study materials:

CONTENT	AAT	
	Text	Kit
Electronic version of the book	✓	✓
Progress tests with instant answers	✓	
Mock assessments online	✓	✓
Material updates	✓	✓

How to access your online resources

Kaplan Financial students will already have a MyKaplan account and these extra resources will be available to you online. You do not need to register again, as this process was completed when you enrolled. If you are having problems accessing online materials, please ask your course administrator.

If you are not studying with Kaplan and did not purchase your book via a Kaplan website, to unlock your extra online resources please go to www.mykaplan.co.uk/addabook (even if you have set up an account and registered books previously). You will then need to enter the ISBN number (on the title page and back cover) and the unique pass key number contained in the scratch panel below to gain access. You will also be required to enter additional information during this process to set up or confirm your account details.

If you purchased through the Kaplan Publishing website you will automatically receive an e-mail invitation to MyKaplan. Please register your details using this email to gain access to your content. If you do not receive the e-mail or book content, please contact Kaplan Publishing.

Your Code and Information

This code can only be used once for the registration of one book online. This registration and your online content will expire when the final sittings for the examinations covered by this book have taken place. Please allow one hour from the time you submit your book details for us to process your request.

Please scratch the film to access your unique code.

Please be aware that this code is case-sensitive and you will need to include the dashes within the passcode, but not when entering the ISBN.

PUBLISHING

CONTENTS

	Page
Index to questions and answers	P.4
Assessment technique	P.10
Unit specific information	P.11
Kaplan's recommended revision approach	P.13
Tax rates and allowances	P.16
Tax administration	P.18

Practice questions	1
Answers to practice questions	79
Mock assessment questions	163
Mock assessment answers	175

Features in this exam kit

In addition to providing a wide ranging bank of real assessment style questions, we have also included in this kit:

- unit specific information and advice on assessment technique
- our recommended approach to make your revision for this particular unit as effective as possible.

You will find a wealth of other resources to help you with your studies on the Kaplan and AAT websites:

www.mykaplan.co.uk

www.aat.org.uk/

Quality and accuracy are of the utmost importance to us so if you spot an error in any of our products, please send an email to mykaplanreporting@kaplan.com with full details, or follow the link to the feedback form in MyKaplan.

Our Quality Coordinator will work with our technical team to verify the error and take action to ensure it is corrected in future editions.

INDEX TO QUESTIONS AND ANSWERS

INCOME TAX AND CORPORATION TAX

		Page number	
		Question	**Answer**
Capital and revenue expenditure			
1	Giles	1	79
2	Philip	2	79
3	Brown	2	80
4	Badges of trade	2	80
Adjustment of profits			
5	Finn	3	82
6	Flush Ltd	5	83
7	Jamie	5	83
8	Crush Ltd	6	84
9	Rebecca	7	85
10	Armadillo	8	85
11	Benabi	8	86
12	Franklin Ltd	10	87
13	Silvain, Alice, Lucille and Pascal	10	88
Capital allowances			
14	Broad Ltd	11	89
15	Well Ltd	13	90
16	Pinker Ltd	14	91
17	Sarah	15	93
18	Dave and Nick	16	94
19	Pirbright Ltd	18	96
Basis of assessment			
20	Kurt	20	97
21	Robert	21	98
22	Javid	22	98
23	Charis	22	99
24	Gordon	22	99
25	Henrietta	23	100
26	Melissa	24	100
27	Antonia	25	101

		Page number	
		Question	Answer
Partnerships			
28	Sue, Will and Terri	26	102
29	Jenny and Harvey	26	102
30	Sally, Barry, Bill and Bea	27	103
31	Alvin, Simon and Theodore	27	103
32	Sian and Ellie	28	103
Trading losses			
33	Nicholas	28	105
34	Joanna	29	106
35	Stilton Ltd	29	106
36	Kane	30	107
37	Green Ltd	30	108
Corporation tax computation			
38	Withers Ltd	31	108
39	Morgan Ltd	31	108
40	Long period of account	32	109
41	Brousse	32	109
42	Taxable total profits	33	110
43	Coupe Ltd	33	110
44	Mercury Ltd	34	111
45	Pangolin Ltd	34	111

CHARGEABLE GAINS

Exempt assets			
46	Debrel	35	112
47	Birch	35	112
48	Rose	35	112
49	Larch	36	112
50	Arkwright	36	113

		Page number	
		Question	**Answer**
Chargeable gain computations			
51	Chargeable gain computations	36	113
52	Wendy	37	113
53	Sylvester Ltd	37	114
54	Rest Ltd	37	115
55	XYZ Ltd	38	115
56	Livingstone Ltd	38	116
57	Stan	39	116
58	Topham Ltd	39	117
59	Sybile	39	117
60	Rizwan	40	118
61	Karen, Ben and Sarah	40	118
Disposal of shares			
62	Puck Ltd	41	120
63	Piston Ltd	42	121
64	Dream Ltd	44	122
65	Batman Ltd	45	123
66	Shelbyville Ltd	46	124
67	James	47	125
68	Goodwin	48	126
Capital gains – Reliefs			
69	Susan and Rachel	49	127
70	Malcolm and Jeremy	50	128
71	Availability of reliefs	51	129
72	Oliver Ltd	51	129
73	John, Paul, George and Ringo	51	130
74	Norman	52	131
75	Harry and Briony	53	132
76	Cheryl	54	133
77	Allyn and Simon	54	133
78	Evan, Zak and Lilia	55	134
79	Ophelia, Georgia and Sid	55	134

NATIONAL INSURANCE CONTRIBUTIONS

		Page number	
		Question	Question
Self-employed individuals			
80	Jenny and Jack	56	135
81	Carter	57	136
82	Ivor	57	136
83	Jake, Sue and Pete	57	137
84	Thomas and Suzanne	58	137
85	Amelie and Alexander	58	138

CURRENT TAX RELIEFS AND OTHER TAX ISSUES

R&D tax credits and IR35			
86	Barry	59	138
87	Caitlin	59	139
88	Joe	59	139
89	Iris	60	140

SELF-ASSESSMENT

Payment dates			
90	Individual's payment dates	60	141
91	Payments on account (POAs)	61	141
92	Company payment dates	61	142
93	Due dates	61	143
94	Company due dates	62	143

		Page number	
		Question	*Answer*
Administration, penalties and ethical standards			
95	Irfan	62	144
96	Compliance checks and appeals	63	146
97	Nagina	64	147
98	Penalties	64	147
99	Maninder	65	148
100	Janet	65	149
101	Ethical rules (1)	65	150
102	Ethical rules (2)	66	151
103	Client advice	66	151
104	AAT student	67	151
105	Nasheen	67	152
106	Tax return responsibility	67	152
107	Laredo	68	153
Written questions			
108	Malik	68	154
109	Bamboo Ltd	69	154
110	Sara	69	155
111	Charlie	69	155
112	Melanie	70	156
113	Charlotte	70	156
114	Sophia	71	157
Tax returns			
115	Jordan	71	159
116	Bintou	74	160
117	Lynne and Shirley Peters	76	161

ANSWER ENHANCEMENTS

We have added the following enhancements to the answers in this exam kit:

Key answer tips

Some answers include key answer tips to help your understanding of each question.

Tutorial note

Some answers include tutorial notes to explain some of the technical points in more detail.

ASSESSMENT TECHNIQUE

- **Do not skip any of the material** in the syllabus.

- Read each question very carefully.

- **Double-check your answer** before committing yourself to it.

- Answer **every** question – if you do not know an answer to a multiple choice question or true/false question, you don't lose anything by guessing. Think carefully before you **guess**.

- If you are answering a multiple-choice question, **eliminate first those answers that you know are wrong**. Then choose the most appropriate answer from those that are left.

- **Don't panic** if you realise you've answered a question incorrectly. Getting one question wrong will not mean the difference between passing and failing.

Computer-based assessments – tips

- Do not attempt a CBA until you have **completed all study material** relating to it.

- On the AAT website there is a CBA demonstration. It is **ESSENTIAL** that you attempt this before your real CBA. You will become familiar with how to move around the CBA screens and the way that questions are formatted, increasing your confidence and speed in the actual assessment.

- Be sure you understand how to use the **software** before you start the assessment. If in doubt, ask the assessment centre staff to explain it to you.

- Questions are **displayed on the screen** and answers are entered using keyboard and mouse. At the end of the assessment, you are given a certificate showing the result you have achieved unless some manual marking is required for the assessment.

- In addition to the traditional multiple-choice question type, CBAs will also contain **other types of questions**, such as number entry questions, drag and drop, true/false, pick lists or drop down menus or hybrids of these.

- In some CBAs you may have to type in complete computations or written answers.

- You need to be sure you **know how to answer questions** of this type before you sit the real assessment, through practice.

KAPLAN PUBLISHING

UNIT SPECIFIC INFORMATION

THE ASSESSMENT

FORMAT OF THE ASSESSMENT

Students will be assessed by computer-based assessment.

In any one assessment, students may not be assessed on all content, or on the full depth or breadth of a piece of content. The content assessed may change over time to ensure validity of assessment, but all assessment criteria will be tested over time.

The learning outcomes for this unit are as follows:

	Learning outcome	Weighting
1	Complete tax returns for sole traders and partnerships and prepare supporting tax computations	29%
2	Complete tax returns for limited companies and prepare supporting tax computations	19%
3	Provide advice on the UK's tax regime and its impact on sole traders, partnerships and limited companies	15%
4	Advise business clients on tax reliefs, and their responsibilities and their agent's responsibilities in reporting taxation to HM Revenue & Customs.	19%
5	Prepare tax computations for the sale of capital assets	18%
	Total	100%

Time allowed

2 hours

PASS MARK

The pass mark for all AAT CBAs is 70%.

 Always keep your eye on the clock and make sure you attempt all questions!

DETAILED SYLLABUS

The detailed syllabus and study guide written by the AAT can be found at:

www.aat.org.uk/

REFERENCE MATERIAL

Reference material is provided in this assessment. During your assessment you will be able to access reference material through a series of clickable links on the right of every task. These will produce pop-up windows which can be moved or closed.

ASSESSMENT GUIDANCE

- Some questions ask that answers be calculated to the nearest £. Some answers may require learners to calculate to the nearest £ and pence. If the question does not give any instructions then either method is acceptable and the computer will accept both.

- Some questions have scroll bars at the side. It is important that learners scroll down and do not miss out parts of questions.

- Where free text written answers are required, learners are supplied with a box to type their answers. This scrolls down as far as is necessary to accommodate the learner's answer.

- It is very important to read questions carefully. Common errors which have occurred in the assessments are:

  (i)   Not spotting when amounts are given monthly and not annually

  (ii)   Misreading dates

  (iii)   Being unable to work out the number of months in a period when time apportionment is required (e.g. for a partnership 'salary').

- Tasks involving basis period rules or loss relief rules are very badly answered.

- Capital allowance computations – this is a vital area. Tasks involving long or short periods or a cessation are often poorly answered.

KAPLAN'S RECOMMENDED REVISION APPROACH

QUESTION PRACTICE IS THE KEY TO SUCCESS

Success in professional examinations relies upon you acquiring a firm grasp of the required knowledge at the tuition phase. In order to be able to do the questions, knowledge is essential.

However, the difference between success and failure often hinges on your assessment technique on the day and making the most of the revision phase of your studies.

The **Kaplan study text** is the starting point, designed to provide the underpinning knowledge to tackle all questions. However, in the revision phase, poring over text books is not the answer.

Kaplan pocket notes are designed to help you quickly revise a topic area; however you then need to practise questions. There is a need to progress to assessment style questions as soon as possible, and to tie your assessment technique and technical knowledge together.

The importance of question practice cannot be over-emphasised.

The recommended approach below is designed by expert tutors in the field, in conjunction with their knowledge of the chief assessor and the sample assessment.

You need to practise as many questions as possible in the time you have left.

OUR AIM

Our aim is to get you to the stage where you can attempt assessment questions confidently, to time, in a closed book environment, with no supplementary help (i.e. to simulate the real assessment experience).

Practising your assessment technique is also vitally important for you to assess your progress and identify areas of weakness that may need more attention in the final run up to the real assessment.

In order to achieve this we recognise that initially you may feel the need to practise some questions with open book help.

Good assessment technique is vital.

THE KAPLAN REVISION PLAN

Stage 1: Assess areas of strength and weakness

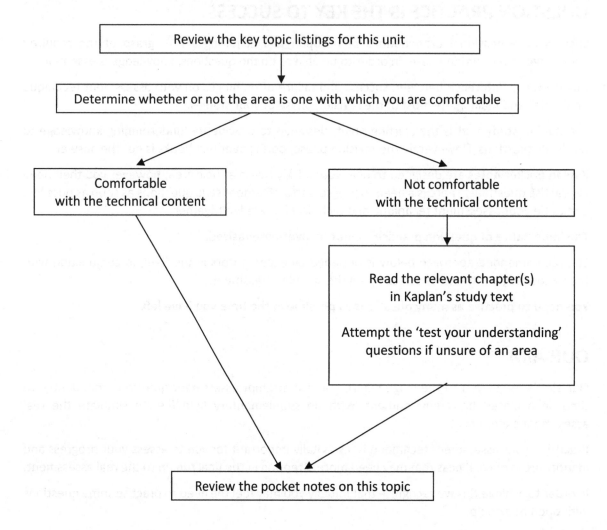

Stage 2: Practise questions

Follow the order of revision of topics as presented in this kit and attempt the questions in the order suggested.

Try to avoid referring to study texts and your notes and the model answer until you have completed your attempt.

Review your attempt with the model answer and assess how much of the answer you achieved.

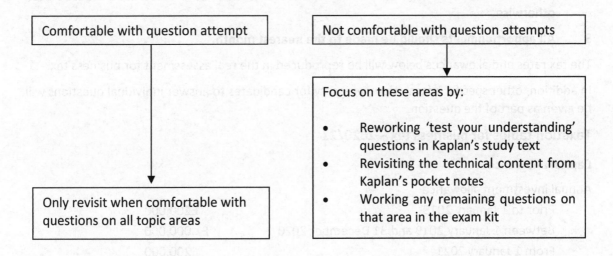

Stage 3: Final pre-real assessment revision

We recommend that you **attempt at least one two hour mock assessment** containing a set of previously unseen real assessment standard questions.

Attempt the mock CBA online in timed, closed book conditions to simulate the real assessment experience.

You will find a mock CBA for this unit at www.mykaplan.co.uk

TAX RATES AND ALLOWANCES

Throughout this exam kit:

1   You should assume that the tax rates and allowances for the tax year 2020/21 and for the Financial Year to 31 March 2021 will continue to apply for the foreseeable future unless you are instructed otherwise.

2   Calculations and workings of tax liability should be made to the nearest £ unless stated otherwise.

3   All apportionments should be made to the nearest month.

The tax rates and allowances below will be reproduced in the real assessment for business tax.

In addition, other specific information necessary for candidates to answer individual questions will be given as part of the question.

Taxation tables for business tax – 2020/21

Capital allowances

Annual investment allowance

Prior to 1 January 2019	£200,000
Between 1 January 2019 and 31 December 2020	£1,000,000
From 1 January 2021	£200,000

Plant and machinery writing down allowance

Assets other than motor cars	18%

Motor cars

CO_2 emissions up to 50 g/km	100%
CO_2 emissions between 51 and 110 g/km	18%
CO_2 emissions over 110 g/km – Prior to 1 April 2019 / 6 April 2019	8%
CO_2 emissions over 110 g/km – From 1 April 2019 / 6 April 2019	6%

Capital gains

Annual exempt amount	£12,300
Basic rate	10%
Higher rate	20%
Business asset disposal relief rate	10%
Investors' relief rate	10%
Business asset disposal relief lifetime allowance	£1,000,000
Investors' relief lifetime allowance	£10,000,000

National Insurance rates

Class 2 contributions:

Small profits threshold	£3.05 per week
	£6,475 p.a.

Class 4 contributions:

Main rate	9%
Additional rate	2%
Lower profits limit	£9,500
Upper profits limit	£50,000

Trading allowance

This allowance is available to individuals only	£1,000

Corporation tax

Financial year	2020	2019
All profits and gains	19%	19%

TAX ADMINISTRATION

This is a useful summary. Much of the following information is given in the Business Tax reference material provided in your assessment.

Self-assessment – individuals

Election/claim	Time limit	For 2020/21
Pay days for income tax and class 4 NICs	1st instalment: 31 January in the tax year	31 January 2021
	2nd instalment: 31 July following the end of tax year	31 July 2021
	Balancing payment: 31 January following the end of tax year	31 January 2022
Pay day for class 2 NICs	31 January following the end of the tax year	31 January 2022
Pay day for CGT	31 January following the end of tax year	31 January 2022
Filing dates If return issued more than 3 months before the filing date	Paper return: 31 October following end of tax year	31 October 2021
	Electronic return: 31 January following end of tax year	31 January 2022
If return issued less than 3 months before the filing date	3 months from the date of issue of the return	
Retention of records – Business records	5 years from 31 January following end of the tax year	31 January 2027
– Personal records	12 months from 31 January following end of the tax year	31 January 2023
HMRC right of repair	9 months from date the return was filed	
Taxpayer's right to amend a return	12 months from 31 January following end of the tax year	31 January 2023
Repayment relief claim	4 years following end of the tax year	5 April 2025
HMRC can open a compliance check	12 months from submission of the return	
Taxpayer's right of appeal against an assessment	30 days from the date of the assessment – appeal in writing	

Self-assessment – companies

Election/claim	Time limit
Pay day for companies which are not large	9 months and one day after the end of the accounting period
Pay day for large companies	Instalments due on 14th day of: – 7th, 10th, 13th, and 16th month **after the start** of the accounting period
Filing dates	Later of: – 12 months from the end of the accounting period – 3 months from the issue of a notice to deliver a corporation tax return
Companies repayment relief claim	4 years from the end of the accounting period
Retention of records	6 years from the end of the accounting period
HMRC can open a compliance check	12 months from submission of the return
Taxpayer's right of appeal against an assessment	30 days from the date of the assessment – appeal in writing

PENALTIES

Individuals and companies

Offence		Penalty
Incorrect return	% of revenue lost (tax unpaid as a result of the error)	Maximum %
	Mistake	0
	Failure to take reasonable care	30
	Deliberate understatement	70
	Deliberate understatement with concealment	100
	Penalties can be reduced for taxpayer disclosure	

PENALTIES (CONT)

Offence		Penalty
Late notification	% of tax unpaid on 31 January following tax year end for individuals and 12 months after the end of the accounting period for companies Percentages as for incorrect returns Penalties can be reduced for taxpayer disclosure	
Failure to keep records	Per tax year or accounting period	£3,000

Individuals

Late payment of tax (cumulative)	% of tax unpaid on 31 January following tax year end	
	More than 30 days late	5% of tax overdue
	More than 6 months late	Further 5% of tax overdue
	More than 12 months late	Further 5% of tax overdue

Late filing (cumulative)	Filed after due date	£100 fixed penalty
	Filed more than 3 months late	£10 per day for up to 90 days (max £900) in addition to fixed penalty
	Filed more than 6 months late	5% of tax due plus above penalties (min £300)
	More than 12 months late where withholding information was:	The penalties above plus additional:
	– not deliberate	5% of tax due (min £300)
	– deliberate but no concealment	70% tax due (min £300)
	– deliberate with concealment	100% tax due (min £300)

Companies

Late filing (cumulative)	Less than 3 months late	£100 fixed penalty
	Filed more than 3 months late	£200 fixed penalty
	Filed more than 6 months late	10% of tax due per return
	More than 12 months late	20% of tax due per return

Penalties can be reduced if the taxpayer has a **reasonable excuse**

Section 1

PRACTICE QUESTIONS

INCOME TAX AND CORPORATION TAX

CAPITAL AND REVENUE EXPENDITURE

Key answer tips

Adjustment of profits and determining capital versus revenue expenditure are important areas and likely to be tested. Knowledge of what is treated as capital and what is not is often an area where learners slip up. It is important not to neglect learning facts such as these.

The Business Tax reference material provided in your assessment covers these topics in the sections headed 'Adjustment of profits – sole traders, partnerships and companies' and 'Unincorporated businesses – trading income'.

1 GILES

Giles incurred the following expenditure.

For each item of expenditure, tick the appropriate box to show whether the item is treated as revenue or capital expenditure.

	Revenue	Capital
Decorating an office		
Computer for a salesman		
Office building extension		
Electricity for the quarter to 31 March 2021		
Meal to entertain a customer from Germany		
Fork lift truck for the warehouse		

2 PHILIP

Philip incurred the following expenditure.

For each item of expenditure, tick the appropriate box to show whether the item is treated as revenue or capital expenditure.

	Revenue	Capital
Printer for the office computer		
Water rates		
Legal fees for purchase of a building		

3 BROWN

Brown incurred the following expenditure.

For each item of expenditure, tick the appropriate box to show whether the item is treated as revenue or capital expenditure.

	Revenue	Capital
Repairs to a boiler		
Insurance for motor cars		
Replacement of a severely damaged roof on a newly-purchased warehouse before being able to use the building		
Parking fine incurred by Brown		

4 BADGES OF TRADE

Read the following statements. Tick the appropriate box to show whether or not the individual is likely to be considered to be carrying on a trade.

	Carrying on a trade	Not carrying on a trade
Fred buys a painting in 2013 for £40,000 and hangs it in his home. In 2020 he sells the painting for £50,000 as he needs the cash to pay for a new house.		
Franz regularly buys items in charity shops and then sells them soon after on online auction sites for a higher price. He estimates that each week he has a cash profit of £250 from the sales.		
Each month Jason buys an old car and then repairs it prior to selling it at a profit. He has rented a lock up garage to carry out this work. He uses the money he receives from selling a car to buy the next car.		

ADJUSTMENT OF PROFITS

Key answer tips

Adjustment of profits questions may include a computation starting from the accounting profit where you will need to adjust for disallowed expenses. It is important to carefully read the question and consider each item to decide whether it is allowable or not.

5   **FINN**

Finn is self-employed and has a business making widgets.

The business has the following statement of profit or loss for the year ended 31 March 2021:

	£	£
Turnover		1,360,250
Less: Cost of sales		(776,780)
Gross profit		583,470
Wages and salaries	147,280	
Rent and rates	65,280	
Repairs	30,760	
Advertising and entertaining	27,630	
Accountancy and legal costs	16,260	
Motor expenses	38,000	
Leasing costs	8,000	
Telephone and office costs	15,200	
Depreciation	26,525	
Other expenses	101,265	
		(476,200)
Net profit		107,270

Additional information:

1   Repairs include:

	£
Redecorating Finn's flat	10,000
Decorating business premises	12,000

2   Advertising and entertaining includes:

	£
Gifts to customers:	
Food hampers costing £25 each	1,050
Pens carrying the business's logo, costing £5 each	400
Sponsorship of local charity fete	5,300

3   Motor expenses comprise the running costs of:

	£
Delivery vans	22,000
Sales representative's car	10,000
Finn's car which is 50% used for private mileage	6,000

4   Leasing costs of £8,000 are for the sales representative's car which has CO_2 emissions of 135g/km.

5   Other expenses include:

	£
Donation to Children in Need (a national charity)	500
Health and safety fine	400

6   Capital allowances have already been calculated at £21,070.

Calculate Finn's tax adjusted trading profits for the year ended 31 March 2021 using the following pro forma.

Where an item does not require adjustment insert a 0. Where an item is to be deducted from net profit, include it in brackets.

	£	£
Net profit		107,270
Wages and salaries		
Rent and rates		
Repairs		
Advertising and entertaining		
Accountancy and legal costs		
Motor expenses		
Leasing costs		
Telephone and office costs		
Depreciation		
Other expenses		
	———	
		———
Capital allowances		
		———
Adjusted net profit		
		———

6   FLUSH LTD

Flush Ltd incurred the following expenditure.

For each item of expenditure, tick the appropriate box(es) to show whether the item will be treated as allowable or disallowable in the company's adjustment of trading profits computation, and whether or not capital allowances (CAs) will be available.

	Allowable	Disallowable	CAs available
Decorating an office			
Computer for a salesman			
Office building extension			
Electricity for the quarter to 31 March 2021			
Fork lift truck for the warehouse			
Meal to entertain a customer from Italy			
Printer for the office computer			
Interest payable on a loan to purchase an investment property			
Dividends payable			
Costs of a fraud carried out by a director. These costs are not covered by insurance.			

7   JAMIE

Jamie's food manufacturing business has the following statement of profit or loss for the year ended 31 March 2021:

	£	£
Turnover		835,280
Less: Cost of sales		(437,528)
Gross profit		397,752
Wages and salaries	165,948	
Rent, rates and insurance	50,100	
Motor expenses	26,250	
Depreciation	40,355	
Other expenses	137,165	
		(419,818)
Net loss		(22,066)

Additional information:

1   Wages and salaries include:

	£
Jamie	28,000
Jamie's wife Sue, who does not work in the business	12,500
Jamie's daughter, Lisa, the Financial Controller of the business	21,425

2   Motor expenses comprise the running costs of:

	£
Delivery vans	17,940
Salesman's car	6,060
Jamie's motorbike (30% private use)	2,250

3   Other expenses include:

	£
Entertaining customers	625
Entertaining staff (Christmas party)	300
Cost of recipe books given to customers, each with the business logo clearly showing, costing £12.50 each	750
Cost of staff training	1,015

4   Jamie had taken two tins of caviar to eat at home. He paid the business the cost price of £50 each for these tins. Their selling price was £200 each.

5   Capital allowances have already been calculated at £42,236.

Calculate Jamie's tax adjusted trading profits for the year ended 31 March 2021.

8   CRUSH LTD

Crush Ltd incurred the following expenditure.

For each item of expenditure, tick the appropriate box(es) to show whether the item will be treated as allowable or disallowable in the company's adjustment of trading profits computation, and whether or not capital allowances (CAs) will be available.

	Allowable	Disallowable	CAs available
Water rates			
Building insurance			
Replacement of factory machinery			
Replacement of a severely damaged roof on an office building			
Insurance for motor cars			
Parking fine incurred by an employee			

9   REBECCA

Rebecca runs a beauty salon and lives in the small flat above the salon.

Her business has the following statement of profit or loss for the year ended 31 March 2021:

	£	£
Turnover		351,822
Less: Cost of sales		(208,178)
Gross profit		143,644
Profit on sale of equipment		1,280
		144,924
Professional fees	980	
Impaired debts	1,540	
Repairs and maintenance	340	
Depreciation	7,424	
Heating	2,240	
Rent, rates and insurance	12,000	
Motor expenses	7,780	
Wages and salaries	30,936	
Telephone and office costs	742	
Miscellaneous expenses	1,778	
		(65,760)
Net profit		79,164

Additional information:

1   Professional fees comprise:

	£
Accountancy fees	720
Payroll fees	260

2   Impaired debts comprise:

	£
Increase in specific impaired debt provision	800
Increase in general impaired debt provision	268
Trade debts written off	672
Trade debts recovered	(200)

3   Rent, rates and insurance include expenses relating to the flat where Rebecca lives of £3,000.

4   Motor expenses comprise the running costs of:

	£
Van expenses (van used by Rebecca exclusively for the business)	5,090
Car expenses (car used by Rebecca exclusively for private purposes)	2,690

5   Wages and salaries include Rebecca's drawings of £18,000.

6   Miscellaneous expenses include:

	£
Gifts of diaries to customers costing £7 each and bearing the logo of the business	798
Parking fines incurred by Rebecca in the van	280

7   One of your colleagues has calculated Rebecca's capital allowances to be £11,642.

Calculate Rebecca's tax adjusted trading profits for the year ended 31 March 2021.

10 ARMADILLO

Armadillo is self-employed and his business has made a profit of £34,890 in the year ended 31 March 2021.

This is after the inclusion of the following expenditure:

- Depreciation of £2,345.

- Motor expenses of £4,788. This relates equally to two cars both of which are used 50% for private journeys, one by Armadillo and one by an employee.

- Staff Christmas party of £2,570, which worked out at £257 per head.

- Gift aid donation of £34.

- Wages to Armadillo's wife of £19,000. Other members of staff with the same job in the business are paid £14,500.

- Capital allowances have been calculated at £3,460.

Calculate Armadillo's tax adjusted trading profits for the year ended 31 March 2021.

11 BENABI

Benabi's business has the following statement of profit or loss for the year ended 31 March 2021:

	£	£
Turnover		424,800
Less: Cost of sales		(280,900)
Gross profit		143,900
Wages and salaries	67,400	
Rent, rates and insurance	8,100	
Repairs to plant	3,456	
Advertising and entertaining	6,098	
Accountancy and legal costs	2,400	
Motor expenses	5,555	
Depreciation	8,001	
Telephone and office costs	3,699	
Other expenses	5,702	
		(110,411)
Net profit		33,489

Additional information:

1 Wages and salaries include:

	£
Benabi	6,000
Benabi's wife, who works in the marketing department	8,000

2　Advertising and entertaining includes:

	£
Gifts to customers:	
Boxes of chocolates, costing £5 each	1,250
Calendars carrying the business's logo, costing £10 each	400
Staff Christmas party for 8 employees	480

3　Motor expenses include:

	£
Sales manager's car	820
Benabi's car which is only used for private mileage	1,100

4　Other expenses include:

	£
Cost of staff training	490
Subscription to a local gym for Benabi	220

5　Capital allowances have already been calculated at £9,955.

Calculate Benabi's tax adjusted trading profits for the year ended 31 March 2021 using the following pro forma.

Where an item does not require adjustment insert a 0. Where an item is to be deducted from net profit, include it in brackets.

	£	£
Net profit		33,489
Wages and salaries		
Rent, rates and insurance		
Repairs to plant		
Advertising and entertaining		
Accountancy and legal costs		
Motor expenses		
Depreciation		
Telephone and office costs		
Other expenses		
	——	
		——
Capital allowances		
		——
Adjusted net profit		
		——

12 FRANKLIN LTD

Franklin Ltd commenced to trade on 1 April 2020 and incurred the following expenditure in its first year of trading to 31 March 2021.

For each item of expenditure, tick the appropriate box to show whether the item will be treated as allowable or disallowable in the adjustment of trading profits computation.

	Allowable	Disallowable
Donation of £500 to Oxfam (a national charity)		
Donation of £100 to the local animal hospital		
Advertising costs incurred in January 2020		
Entertaining prospective customers in February 2020		
Dividends paid to shareholders on 2 January 2021		

13 SILVAIN, ALICE, LUCILLE AND PASCAL

Silvain, Alice, Lucille and Pascal have the following trading income and expenses for the year ended 31 March 2021. All expenses were allowable for tax purposes.

	Silvain	Alice	Lucille	Pascal
	£	£	£	£
Trading income	860	690	3,750	6,300
Expenses	300	740	930	3,080

Complete the following table to show whether each taxpayer should use the trading allowance. Where relevant, show whether the allowance would be given automatically, whether the taxpayer should elect to receive the allowance or whether he/she should elect not to claim the allowance. Calculate the taxable trading income for each taxpayer. Enter 0 if there would be no taxable trading income.

	Silvain	Alice	Lucille	Pascal
Should use the trading allowance				
Given automatically				
Elect to receive				
Elect not to receive				
Taxable trading income (£)				

CAPITAL ALLOWANCES

Key answer tips

There is likely to be a task in the assessment that will test capital allowances. This may include a capital allowances computation to complete. There is a detailed pro forma computation included in the Business Tax reference material provided in your assessment in the section headed 'Capital allowances on plant and machinery'. Note that this pro forma has separate columns dealing with additions qualifying for AIA and for FYA. The answers in this exam kit use one column which is useful to save space. Either approach is acceptable.

You must learn the detailed rules regarding the treatment of different types of asset, especially cars, as you may be assessed on the theory behind the capital allowance rules in a separate part of the task.

You must also be able to deal with short or long accounting periods and the period leading up to the cessation of the business.

You need to be able to deal with periods straddling the increase in the AIA from £200,000 to £1,000,000 from 1 January 2019, and the subsequent decrease from £1,000,000 to £200,000 from 1 January 2021. For businesses with a chargeable period straddling this date the maximum AIA will be time apportioned.

In addition, you may have to deal with periods straddling the decrease in the WDA for cars with CO_2 emissions of more than 110g/km from 8% to 6% from 6 April 2019 (1 April 2019 for companies), which will also require time apportionment.

14 BROAD LTD

Broad Ltd has the following non-current asset information for the year ended 31 December 2020:

	£
Balances brought forward as at 1 January 2020:	
General pool	140,000
Special rate pool	26,000
Additions in May and June 2020:	
Machinery	1,020,000
Finance Director's car (Citroen)	34,000
Sales Director's car (BMW)	32,000
Plant	10,000
Disposals in June 2020:	
Machinery (Cost £10,000)	10,200
Sales Director's car (Vauxhall) (cost £21,000)	13,800

The CO$_2$ emissions of the cars are:

Citroen   46g/km
BMW   105g/km
Vauxhall   160g/km

All the cars are used 75% for business and 25% privately.

Calculate Broad Ltd's total capital allowances and show the balances to carry forward to the next accounting period.

Use the grid provided for your answer. You have been given more space than you need.

15   WELL LTD

Well Ltd has provided the following information for the year ended 31 March 2021:

	£
Balances brought forward as at 1 April 2020:	
General pool	134,500
Special rate pool	36,000
Additions in May 2020:	
Machinery	844,167
Finance Director's car (Peugeot) (CO_2 emissions 102g/km)	34,500
Disposals in September 2020:	
Machinery (Cost £12,000)	10,000
Finance Director's car (Toyota) (Cost £13,200) (CO_2 emissions 145g/km)	11,800

Both cars are used 40% privately.

Calculate Well Ltd's total capital allowances and show the balances to carry forward to the next accounting period.

Use the grid provided for your answer. You have been given more space than you need.

16 PINKER LTD

(a) Pinker Ltd changed its accounting date and has sent you the following information about its non-current assets for the five months accounting period ended 31 December 2020.

Balances brought forward as at 1 August 2020:

General pool	£345,980
Special rate pool	£23,000

In August 2020 the company bought plant for £539,000, a car with CO_2 emissions of 103g/km for £18,000, and a car with CO_2 emissions of 45g/km for £13,790.

Calculate Pinker Ltd's total capital allowances and show the balances to carry forward to the next accounting period.

Use the grid provided for your answer. You have been given more space than you need.

(b)   Which of the following statements about short life assets are true and which are false?

	True	False
Short life assets have a maximum life of 6 years		
Annual investment allowance should be allocated against additions in the general pool before it is allocated against a short life asset		
Short life assets purchased by X Ltd have a writing down allowance of 18% p.a.		
It is beneficial to claim the short life asset treatment for cars		
Short life asset treatment is compulsory for qualifying assets		

17   SARAH

Sarah's sole trader business has the following non-current asset information for the year ended 31 December 2020:

	£
Balances brought forward as at 1 January 2020:	
General pool	65,100
Sarah's Peugeot car (20% private usage)	14,500
Short life asset (bought in 2016)	7,420
Additions:	
Office furniture	11,000
Van	8,600
Sarah's Toyota car – to be used solely for business purposes	20,000
Plant	15,500
Disposals:	
Office furniture – original cost higher than disposal value	14,200
Sarah's Peugeot car	10,000
Short life asset	1,400

The CO_2 emissions of the vehicles are:

Peugeot	175g/km
Van	130g/km
Toyota	45g/km

Calculate Sarah's total capital allowances and show the balances to carry forward to the next accounting period.

Use the grid provided for your answer. You have been given more space than you need.

18   DAVE AND NICK

(a)   Dave and Nick formed a partnership and started trading on 1 January 2019.

The partnership made the following non-current asset additions in the period ended 31 August 2019:

	£
Plant	7,680
Office furniture	12,450
Car for Dave, 30% private use, CO_2 emissions 155g/km	15,300
Car for Nick, 40% private use, CO_2 emissions 100g/km	10,200

Calculate the partnership's total capital allowances and show the balances to carry forward to the next accounting period.

Use the grid provided for your answer. You have been given more space than you need.

(b)   The partnership did not do well and ceased to trade on 31 August 2020. Further plant had been bought in March 2020 costing £10,000.

When the trade ceased all the plant and furniture was sold for £22,000. Dave and Nick took over their cars at market value of £12,500 and £7,500 respectively.

Calculate the partnership's total capital allowances for the final period of trading.

Use the grid provided for your answer. You have been given more space than you need.

19 PIRBRIGHT LTD

Pirbright Ltd has the following non-current asset information for the year ended 30 June 2020:

		£
Balances brought forward as at 1 July 2019:		
General pool		81,000
Special rate pool		28,900
Additions:		
1 May 2020	Machinery	640,000
11 May 2020	Hyundai car	21,000
1 June 2020	Managing Director's Jaguar car	38,600

			Proceeds
			£

Disposals:

| 26 February 2020 | Machinery | Cost £22,000 | 11,250 |
| 1 June 2020 | Managing Director's Lexus car | Cost £30,000 | 15,400 |

The CO$_2$ emissions of the vehicles are:

Hyundai	30g/km
Jaguar	142g/km
Lexus	155g/km

The Managing Director used the Jaguar and Lexus 30% privately.

Calculate Pirbright Ltd's total capital allowances and show the balances to carry forward to the next accounting period.

Use the grid provided for your answer. You have been given more space than you need.

BASIS OF ASSESSMENT

Key answer tips

Basis of assessment for new, ongoing and ceasing businesses as well as partnerships (see the next section) is an important topic. The effect of a change in accounting date can also be tested. Tasks may be broken into a number of smaller tasks rather than one large one.

These rules are covered in the Business Tax reference material provided in your assessment in the sections headed 'Sole traders – basis periods', 'Sole traders – change of accounting date' and 'Partnerships'.

It is important to use an appropriate amount of time in the assessment for these tasks, and not to rush your answer.

20   KURT

Kurt started trading on 1 October 2017. He prepares his accounts to 30 June each year.

His tax adjusted trading profits were calculated as follows:

	£
Period to 30 June 2018	22,500
Year to 30 June 2019	43,200
Year to 30 June 2020	47,000

(a)   The tax year in which he started trading was:

    A   2016/17

    B   2018/19

    C   2017/18

    D   2019/20

(b)   His taxable profits in his first tax year of trading were:

    A   £15,000

    B   £15,750

    C   £22,500

    D   £17,500

(c)   His taxable profits in his second tax year of trading were:

    A   £43,200

    B   £39,900

    C   £33,300

    D   £22,500

(d)   His taxable profits in his third tax year of trading were:

    A   £47,000

    B   £43,200

    C   £44,150

    D   £46,050

(e)   His overlap profits were:

(f)   Unless Kurt changes his accounting date, his overlap profits are deducted from:

    A   his profits in the second tax year of trading

    B   the profits in the final tax year of trading

    C   the profits in the first tax year of trading

    D   any profits chosen by Kurt

21   ROBERT

Robert started trading on 1 January 2019. He prepares his accounts to 31 October each year.

His tax adjusted trading profits were calculated as follows:

	£
10 months to 31 October 2019	32,000
Year ended 31 October 2020	45,000
Year ended 31 October 2021	87,000

(a)   His taxable profits for 2018/19 were:

    A   £32,000

    B   £9,600

    C   £39,500

    D   £45,000

(b)   His taxable profits for 2019/20 were:

    A   £32,000

    B   £45,000

    C   £39,500

    D   £41,150

(c)   His taxable profits for 2020/21 will be:

    A   £32,000

    B   £45,000

    C   £87,000

    D   £62,500

(d)   His overlap profits were:

22   JAVID

Javid starts trading on 1 January 2020 and draws up his first set of accounts to 31 May 2021.

The period for which his profits will be assessed for the second tax year will be:

A   1 January 2020 to 5 April 2020

B   1 January 2020 to 31 December 2020

C   6 April 2020 to 5 April 2021

D   12 months to 31 May 2021

23   CHARIS

Charis commenced business as a sole trader on 1 January 2020 and prepared her first set of accounts for the period ended 28 February 2021.

In the 14-month period ended 28 February 2021 her tax adjusted trading profit was £21,000.

Her second set of accounts will be for the year ended 28 February 2022 when the tax adjusted trading profits are expected to be £24,000.

What is Charis's trading income assessment for the tax year 2020/21?

A   £21,000

B   £18,000

C   £18,500

D   £24,000

24   GORDON

Gordon ceased trading on 30 November 2020.

Until then, he had been preparing his accounts to 30 June each year.

The tax adjusted trading profits in the final periods of trading were as follows:

	£
Year to 30 June 2019	132,000
Year to 30 June 2020	120,000
Period to 30 November 2020	56,000

He had overlap profits from commencement of trade of £22,000.

(a)   The tax year in which he ceased trading was:

A   2018/19

B   2019/20

C   2020/21

D   2021/22

(b)   His taxable profits in his penultimate tax year of trading were:

     A   £132,000

     B   £120,000

     C   £56,000

     D   £123,000

(c)   His taxable profits in his final tax year of trading were:

     A   £176,000

     B   £154,000

     C   £34,000

     D   £56,000

(d)   When Gordon prepares his final capital allowances computation for the period to 30 November 2020, which of the following types of allowance may be available?

     A   Annual investment allowance

     B   Writing down allowance

     C   First year allowance

     D   Balancing allowance

25   HENRIETTA

Henrietta started trading on 1 February 2019. She prepares her first set of accounts to 31 May 2020 and then to 31 May each year.

Her tax adjusted trading profits were calculated as follows:

	£
Period to 31 May 2020	7,860
Year to 31 May 2021	8,820
Year to 31 May 2022	15,000

(a)   The tax year in which she started trading was:

     A   2020/21

     B   2017/18

     C   2018/19

     D   2019/20

(b)   Her taxable profits in her first tax year of trading were:

     A   £7,860

     B   £3,930

     C   £983

     D   £5,895

(c)   Her taxable profits in her second tax year of trading were:

A   £5,895

B   £7,860

C   £8,820

D   £6,877

(d)   Her taxable profits in her third tax year of trading were:

A   £15,000

B   £5,895

C   £8,820

D   £8,333

(e)   Her overlap profits were:

```
┌──────────────────────┐
│                      │
└──────────────────────┘
```

(f)   If Henrietta changes her accounting date to 31 August and prepares accounts to 31 August 2023, which one of the following statements is true?

A   Further overlap profits will be created.

B   Some of the existing overlap profits will be used up.

26   MELISSA

Mellissa ceased trading on 30 June 2021.

Until then, she had been preparing her accounts to 30 September each year.

The tax adjusted trading profits in the final periods of trading were as follows:

	£
Year to 30 September 2019	13,000
Year to 30 September 2020	12,000
Period to 30 June 2021	5,000

She had overlap profits from commencement of trade of £2,000.

(a)   The tax year in which Melissa ceased trading was:

A   2018/19

B   2019/20

C   2020/21

D   2021/22

(b)   Her taxable profits in her penultimate tax year of trading were:

A   £13,000

B   £12,000

C   £15,000

D   £17,000

(c) Her taxable profits in her final tax year of trading were:

    A   £3,000

    B   £12,000

    C   £10,000

    D   £5,000

27 ANTONIA

Antonia, a sole trader, has always prepared her accounts to 31 December. She decides to change her accounting date to 30 September by preparing accounts for the nine-month period to 30 September 2020.

Antonia's tax adjusted profits after capital allowances are as follows:

	£
Year to 31 December 2019	38,000
Period to 30 September 2020	46,000
Year to 30 September 2021	52,000

(a) The tax year of change was:

    A   2021/22

    B   2020/21

    C   2019/20

    D   2018/19

(b) Antonia's taxable profits for the tax year of change were:

    A   £55,500

    B   £46,000

    C   £52,000

    D   £59,000

(c) What is the latest date that Antonia can give notice of the change of accounting date?

    A   31 January 2021

    B   30 September 2021

    C   31 December 2021

    D   31 January 2022

(d) Which of the following statements about change of accounting date is false?

    A   A partnership cannot change its accounting date

    B   Accounts drawn up to the new accounting date must not exceed 18 months in length

PARTNERSHIPS

28   SUE, WILL AND TERRI

Sue and Will have been in partnership for many years, preparing their accounts to 30 September each year. Their profit sharing ratio was 3:2 respectively.

On 1 April 2020, Terri joined the partnership and the profit sharing ratio was changed to 2:2:1 for Sue, Will and Terri.

For the year ended 30 September 2020, the tax adjusted trading profit was £84,000.

The division of profit would be calculated as:

		Total £	Sue £	Will £	Terri £
Period to:	A	B	C	D	

Options:

B	=	£84,000;	£42,000;	£33,600;	£35,000	
C	=	£50,400;	£42,000;	£21,000;	£16,800;	£25,200; £14,000
D	=	£33,600;	£42,000;	£21,000;	£16,800;	£25,200; £28,000

		Total £	Sue £	Will £	Terri £
Period to:	E	F	G	H	I

Options

F	=	£84,000;	£42,000;	£50,400;	£49,000	
G	=	£42,000;	£33,600;	£16,800;	£14,000;	£25,200; £20,160
H	=	£42,000;	£33,600;	£16,800;	£14,000;	£25,200; £20,160
I	=	£19,600;	£14,000;	£16,800;	£8,400;	£10,080

Insert the appropriate dates in Boxes A and E in the above table.

Choose one number from each of the options above and insert in the appropriate place in the tables above.

29   JENNY AND HARVEY

Jenny and Harvey are in partnership, and have always shared profits equally.

It was then decided that from 1 April 2020 Jenny would be awarded a salary of £40,000 per annum to recognise the extra work that she had taken on.

For the year ended 31 December 2020, the tax adjusted trading profits were £150,000.

Calculate the 2020/21 assessment for each partner.

Jenny	£
Harvey	£

30 SALLY, BARRY, BILL AND BEA

Sally, Barry, Bill and Bea have been in partnership for many years, preparing their accounts to 31 May each year. Their profit sharing ratio was 4:2:2:1 respectively after allowing 5% p.a. interest on capital.

On 1 September 2019, they changed the profit sharing ratio to 4:3:2:2 for Sally, Barry, Bill and Bea respectively and decided to have no more interest on capital.

For the year ended 31 May 2020, the tax adjusted trading profit was £756,000.

The partner's capital balances at the start of the period of account were £80,000, £100,000, £200,000 and £90,000 for Sally, Barry, Bill and Bea respectively.

Show the division of profit for the year ended 31 May 2020.

31 ALVIN, SIMON AND THEODORE

Alvin, Simon and Theodore have been in partnership for many years, preparing their accounts to 31 January each year. Their profit sharing ratio was 5:3:2 respectively.

On 1 August 2020, Theodore retired from the partnership and the profit sharing ratio was changed to 1:1 for Alvin and Simon.

For the year ended 31 January 2021, the tax adjusted trading profit was £52,800.

The division of profit would be calculated as:

	Total £	Alvin £	Simon £	Theodore £
Period to: A	B	C	D	E

Options:

B	=	£52,800;	£30,800;	£26,400;	£22,000		
C	=	£26,400;	£13,200;	£15,400;	£11,000;	£15,840;	£10,560
D	=	£15,840;	£9,240;	£7,920;	£6,600;	£5,940;	£13,200;	£26,400
E	=	£10,560;	£8,360;	£3,080;	£4,400;	£4,620;	£2,640;	£5,280

	Total £	Alvin £	Simon £	Theodore £
Period to: F	G	H	I	

Options:

G	=	£52,800;	£26,400;	£22,000;	£30,800	
H	=	£26,400;	£13,200;	£11,000;	£15,400;	£17,600;	£7,920
I	=	£26,400;	£13,200;	£11,000;	£15,400;	£7,920;	£5,280

Insert the correct dates in Boxes A and F in the above table.

Choose one number from each of the options above and insert in the appropriate place in the tables above.

32   SIAN AND ELLIE

Sian and Ellie have been in partnership for many years, preparing their accounts to 31 July each year. Their profit sharing ratio was 2:1 respectively.

On 1 May 2020, Owen joined the partnership and the profit sharing ratio was changed to 3:2:1 for Sian, Ellie and Owen respectively.

The tax adjusted trading profit was £36,000 for the year ended 31 July 2020, and £60,000 for the year ended 31 July 2021.

What are Owen's assessable profits for 2020/21 and 2021/22?

2020/21	£
2021/22	£

TRADING LOSSES

Key answer tips

There is likely to be a task in the assessment covering losses for sole traders, partnerships and companies. It may be computational, theory based or a combination of the two. It is important that you understand the difference between the rules applicable to sole traders compared with companies. It is possible that both could be tested in one task – so you must be clear as to which set of rules you are applying.

The Business Tax reference material provided in your assessment covers losses in the sections headed 'Trading losses for sole traders and partnerships' and 'Corporation tax – losses'.

33   NICHOLAS

Nicholas, a junior member of the tax department, asks whether the following statements about losses are true or false.

Tick the appropriate box for each statement.

	True	False
A trading loss made by a company can only be offset against trading profits from the same trade when carrying the loss back		
A capital loss made by a company can be offset against trading profits in the year the loss is made and in future years		
A sole trader cannot restrict the amount of loss offset in the current year to preserve the personal allowance		
A sole trader can carry forward a loss for a maximum of four years		

34 JOANNA

Which one of the following statements made by Joanna is correct?

A   A loss made by a sole trader must be relieved against total income in the current tax year.

B   For a loss made by a sole trader to be relieved in the current tax year, it must first have been relieved in the preceding tax year.

C   A loss made by a sole trader can only be relieved against profits of the same trade when carried forward to future years.

D   A loss made by a sole trader can be relieved against total income arising in future years.

35 STILTON LTD

Stilton Ltd has the following results for the two years ended 31 December 2021.

Year ended 31 December	2020	2021
	£	£
Trading profits/(loss)	8,000	(40,000)
Bank interest	1,000	600
Chargeable gain	1,200	Nil
Qualifying charitable donation	150	150

Stilton Ltd wishes to use its trading loss as soon as possible.

(a)   How much loss relief can Stilton Ltd claim against current year profits?   £ ____

(b)   How much loss relief can Stilton Ltd claim against prior year profits?   £ ____

(c)   How much of the loss will then be available to carry forward to future years?   £ ____

(d)   How much of the qualifying charitable donation can be carried forward to future years?   £ ____

(e)   In future years, what can the trading losses carried forward be relieved against?

   A   Total profits before deducting qualifying charitable donations

   B   Trading profit from any trade

   C   Trading profit from the same trade

   D   Taxable total profits

(f)   Cheddar Ltd had a loss for the year ended 30 June 2021, but continued to trade.

   What is the earliest accounting period in which the company could offset the loss?

   A   Year ended 30 June 2020

   B   Year ended 30 June 2019

   C   Year ended 30 June 2018

   D   Year ended 30 June 2017

36 KANE

Kane asks whether the following statements are true or false.

Tick the appropriate box for each statement.

	True	False
A sole trader can offset a capital loss against chargeable gains in the current and/or the previous tax year, in any order		
Offset of current year capital losses is restricted to leave net gains equal to the annual exempt amount		
A sole trader can offset a trading loss against total income in the current and/or the previous tax year, in any order		
For a trading loss made by a company to be relieved in the preceding accounting period, it must first have been relieved in the current accounting period		
Use of trading loss relief by a company can result in wasted qualifying charitable donations		

37 GREEN LTD

Green Ltd has the following results for the year ended 31 March 2021:

	£
Trading profits	175,000
Interest income	30,000
Net chargeable gains	20,000
Qualifying charitable donation	10,000

The company had trading losses brought forward from the previous period of £180,000 and capital losses brought forward of £30,000.

(a)   Assuming that Green Ltd takes advantage of all beneficial claims that can be made, its taxable total profits for the year ended 31 March 2021 are:

   A   £5,000

   B   £10,000

   C   £15,000

   D   £20,000

(b)   The trading loss left to carry forward at 31 March 2021 is: £ ☐

(c)   The capital loss left to carry forward at 31 March 2021 is: £ ☐

(d)   The amount of unrelieved qualifying charitable donation is: £ ☐

CORPORATION TAX COMPUTATION

Key answer tips

There is likely to be a task in the assessment that will cover taxable total profits and corporation tax payable. It may be broken into a number of smaller parts and the questions in this section give practice on the individual parts that may be tested in this task.

The Business Tax reference material provided in your assessment covers corporation tax in the sections headed 'An outline of corporation tax' and 'The calculation of total profits and corporation tax payable'.

Questions on corporation tax payment dates are included in the payment dates section of this exam kit.

38   WITHERS LTD

The Managing Director of Withers Ltd would like to know the basis upon which items are included in a company's corporation tax computation.

Tick the appropriate box for each item to indicate the basis of assessment for corporation tax purposes.

	Accruals basis	Paid/Receipts basis
Qualifying charitable donations		
Trading income		
Rental income		
Interest income		

39   MORGAN LTD

Morgan Ltd draws up a 15 month set of accounts to 31 March 2021.

What corporation tax computations will need to be prepared?

A   One computation for the whole 15 months.

B   Two computations: one for the 12 months to 31 December 2020 and the other for the 3 months to 31 March 2021.

C   Two computations: one for the 3 months to 31 March 2020 and the other for the 12 months to 31 March 2021.

D   Two computations: the company can choose the lengths as long as neither is more than 12 months.

40   LONG PERIOD OF ACCOUNT

When a company has a long period of account that exceeds 12 months, there are rules on how the income and payments should be apportioned between the accounting periods for tax purposes.

Tick the appropriate box for each item to indicate how it will be treated for corporation tax purposes.

	Time apportion	Separate computation	Period in which it arises
Chargeable gains			
Capital allowances			
Trading profits			
Qualifying charitable donations			

41   BROUSSE

Brousse asks whether the following statements are true or false.

Tick the appropriate box for each statement.

	True	False
An individual sole trader with a 15 month period ended 31 March 2021 will have a maximum AIA of £1,050,000 for capital allowance purposes		
Where a car is provided to a director of a company, the director's private use of the car is not relevant when calculating capital allowances		
An individual sole trader preparing a 17 month period of account must calculate two separate capital allowances computations; one for the first 12 months and the second for the balancing period		
A company with a nine month accounting period ending on 31 March 2021 will qualify for a 75% (100% × 9/12) first year allowance in respect of the acquisition of a new low emission car		
An individual sole trader with an 11 month accounting period must time apportion the available FYAs by 11/12 for capital allowance purposes		
The maximum AIA for a sole trader business with an eight month accounting period ending 31 December 2020 is £666,667		

42 TAXABLE TOTAL PROFITS

Which ONE of the following statements is correct in relation to the calculation of TTP?

A   Qualifying charitable donations are deductible on an accruals basis

B   Dividend income should be included in TTP

C   Chargeable gains should be excluded from TTP

D   Brought forward losses are not deductible from TTP

43 COUPE LTD

Coupe Ltd's accounting period is the 15 months ended 31 December 2020.

Its income and payments for the 15 month period are as follows:

	Total	12 months to 30 Sept 2020	3 months to 31 Dec 2020
	£	£	£
Trading income for 15 months ended 31 December 2020	15,750		
Capital allowances (£5,000 for the period ended 30 September 2020, £2,000 for the period ended 31 December 2020)	7,000		
Rental income (£500 per month paid quarterly in advance)	7,500		
Interest income (£200 per month, received annually on 31 December)	3,000		
Chargeable gain on asset sold on 1 January 2020	800		
Donation to a national charity paid on 31 December 2020	1,000		

Allocate the total amounts to each of the chargeable accounting periods in the table above.

If no amount is allocated to a box then insert Nil.

44   MERCURY LTD

Mercury Ltd has the following results for the nine months ended 31 March 2021:

	£
Trading profits	250,000
Dividend income	27,000
Chargeable gains	13,000
Qualifying charitable donation	2,000

Mercury Ltd has trading losses brought forward from the prior period of £35,000 and capital losses brought forward of £22,000.

Calculate Mercury Ltd's corporation tax payable, assuming advantage is taken of all beneficial claims.

45   PANGOLIN LTD

Pangolin Ltd has the following results for the 16 months ended 31 March 2021:

	£
Tax adjusted trading profits	80,000
Rental income	22,000
Chargeable gain on 11 November 2020	61,000
Capital loss on 15 December 2020	53,000
Qualifying charitable donation on 1 July 2020	3,000

The company is not entitled to any capital allowances during this period.

Calculate the total corporation tax liability of Pangolin Ltd for this 16 month trading period.

CHARGEABLE GAINS

Key answer tips

Tasks may cover gains in relation to both individuals and companies and may include questions on chattels, part disposals, chargeable persons, chargeable disposals and connected persons. The task is likely to include a number of smaller questions and may cover a number of different topics, therefore it is important to learn all aspects and ensure you understand them.

It is important to read the questions carefully to ensure that you understand what is being asked and which aspects of chargeable gains are being tested.

The Business Tax reference material provided in your assessment covers chargeable gains rules in the sections headed 'Introduction to chargeable gains', 'Calculation of gains and losses for individuals' and 'Calculation of gains and losses for companies'.

EXEMPT ASSETS

46 DEBREL

Debrel disposed of four assets in 2020/21.

Tick the appropriate box to indicate which disposals are chargeable to capital gains tax and which are exempt assets.

	Chargeable asset	Exempt asset
Dishwasher – sold for £300		
Diamond bracelet – sold for £4,000 (cost £2,500)		
Jaguar car – sold for £70,000		
Exchequer stock – sold for £100,000		

47 BIRCH

Birch disposed of three assets in 2020/21.

Tick the appropriate box to indicate which disposals are chargeable to capital gains tax and which are exempt assets.

	Chargeable asset	Exempt asset
Antique vase – sold for £23,000		
Vintage classic car		
Unquoted shares		

48 ROSE

Rose disposed of three assets in 2020/21.

Tick the appropriate box to indicate which disposals are chargeable to capital gains tax and which are exempt assets.

	Chargeable asset	Exempt asset
Holiday cottage		
Quoted shares in an ISA		
Racehorse		

49   LARCH

Larch disposed of three assets in 2020/21.

Tick the appropriate box to indicate which disposals are chargeable to capital gains tax and which are exempt assets.

	Chargeable asset	Exempt asset
Freehold factory		
Diamond necklace – sold for £17,000		
Racing pigeon		

50   ARKWRIGHT

Arkwright disposed of three assets in 2020/21.

Tick the appropriate box to indicate which disposals are chargeable to capital gains tax and which are exempt assets.

	Chargeable asset	Exempt asset
Quoted shares		
Prize winning greyhound		
Painting by Monet – sold for £300,000		

CHARGEABLE GAIN COMPUTATIONS

51   CHARGEABLE GAIN COMPUTATIONS

For each of the following items affecting the calculation of chargeable gains, tick the appropriate box.

	Applies to companies only	Applies to individuals only	Applies to both companies and individuals
(a) Annual exempt amount			
(b) Indexation allowance			
(c) Rollover relief			
(d) Business asset disposal relief			
(e) Investors' relief			

52 WENDY

Wendy asks whether the following statements are true or false.

Tick the appropriate box for each statement.

	True	False
Indexation allowance cannot create an allowable capital loss for companies		
Indexation allowance can create an allowable capital loss for individuals		
The indexation factor is calculated to two decimal places		
The indexation factor is always calculated using the movement in the retail prices index from the month of expenditure to the month of disposal		
Indexation allowance is calculated for bonus issues in the share pool of a company		

53 SYLVESTER LTD

Sylvester Ltd sold an antique vase in September 2020 for £5,000.

The vase was bought for £10,000 in September 2008.

The indexation factor from September 2008 to December 2017 was 0.273.

The indexation factor from September 2008 to September 2020 was 0.360.

Complete the following computation:

	£
Sale proceeds	
Cost	
Indexation allowance	
Allowable loss	

54 REST LTD

Rest Ltd sold an antique book for £8,000 in December 2020.

It was purchased in December 2010 for £3,000.

The relevant indexation factor is 0.218.

Which of the following is the correct chargeable gain?

A £Nil – it is an exempt asset

B £3,333

C £4,346

D £5,000

55   XYZ LTD

XYZ Ltd sold a building for £250,000 in January 2021.

The building was purchased for £100,000 in April 2009. An extension was built at a cost of £22,000 in May 2013.

In June 2017 repairs to the roof tiles were made costing £12,000

The indexation factor from April 2009 to December 2017 was 0.315

The indexation factor from May 2013 to December 2017 was 0.112

The indexation factor from June 2017 to December 2017 was 0.021

Complete the following computation:

	£
Sale proceeds	
Costs	
Indexation allowance	
Chargeable gain/allowable loss	

56   LIVINGSTONE LTD

Livingstone Ltd owns 50 hectares of land, which it bought in April 1999 for £180,000.

In November 2020, Livingstone Ltd sold 15 hectares for £200,000, when the remaining 35 hectares had a market value of £700,000.

The indexation factor from April 1999 to December 2017 was 0.683.

The indexation factor from April 1999 to November 2020 was 0.808.

Complete the following computation:

	£
Sale proceeds	
Cost	
Indexation allowance	
Chargeable gain	

57 STAN

Stan asks whether the following statements are true or false.

Tick the appropriate box for each statement.

	True	False
An individual disposing of one third of an investment in land must compare one third of the original cost of the land to the sale proceeds received to calculate the chargeable gain		
A company is 100% owned by Mr Black. The company gifts a capital asset to Mr Black's wife. The gift will be a nil gain/nil loss disposal for capital gains purposes		
Stan is connected to his mother, brother, sister-in-law and niece for the purposes of capital gains tax		
Meera owns a painting which cost £12,000 in 2002. She gives it to a charity in 2020 when the painting is worth £50,000. She has a chargeable gain of £38,000		
Fred bought shares in July 2014 costing £17,500. If Fred dies in 2021 when the shares are worth £40,000, his estate will be charged capital gains tax on a gain of £22,500		

58 TOPHAM LTD

Topham Ltd sold a piece of land for £42,000 in November 2020.

The land was bought for £40,000 in September 2014.

The indexation factor from September 2014 to December 2017 was 0.080.

The indexation factor from September 2014 to November 2020 was 0.159.

Complete the following computation:

	£
Sale proceeds	
Cost	
Indexation allowance	
Chargeable gain/allowable loss	

59 SYBILE

Sybile sold two hectares of land for £160,000 in October 2020.

Sybile purchased a 45 hectare plot of land in June 1992 for £560,000. The market value of her remaining 43 hectares in October 2020 was £840,000.

The indexation factor from June 1992 to December 2017 was 0.996.

The indexation factor from June 1992 to October 2020 was 1.138.

Complete the following computation:

	£
Sale proceeds	
Cost	
Indexation allowance	
Chargeable gain/allowable loss	

60   RIZWAN

Rizwan asks whether the following statements are true or false.

Tick the appropriate box for each statement.

	True	False
On the disposal of a non-wasting chattel with gross sale proceeds in excess of £6,000 and cost of less than £6,000, the chargeable gain is calculated using deemed sale proceeds of £6,000		
Wasting chattels are exempt if disposed of by individuals or companies		
On the disposal of a non-wasting chattel with gross sale proceeds in excess of £6,000 and cost of less than £6,000, the chargeable gain cannot exceed: 5/3 × (gross sale proceeds – £6,000)		
On the disposal of a non-wasting chattel at a loss with gross sale proceeds and cost in excess of £6,000, the allowable loss is calculated using deemed sale proceeds of £6,000		

61   KAREN, BEN AND SARAH

(a)   Karen sold 3 chargeable assets in the year.

She made chargeable gains of £6,000 on Asset 1 and £7,000 on Asset 2. She made a capital loss of £4,000 on Asset 3.

What was her net chargeable gain before deducting the annual exempt amount?

Choose from one of the following options:

£Nil;   £9,000;   £13,000;   £12,300;   £700

(b)   Ben sold 2 chargeable assets in the tax year 2020/21, making gains of £9,000 and £3,900 respectively. He had a capital loss brought forward of £4,000 as at 6 April 2020.

What amount of capital losses remain to be carried forward to the tax year 2021/22?

Choose from one of the following options:

£Nil;   £3,400;   £4,000;   £600

(c)   In 2020/21 Sarah made a gain of £23,000 in respect of a warehouse held for investment purposes and £7,300 in respect of a plot of land. She also made a capital loss of £2,000.

She has taxable income of £26,000 and the basic rate band for 2020/21 is £37,500.

What is her capital gains tax liability for the year?   £ _____

DISPOSAL OF SHARES

Key answer tips

There is likely to be a task that will cover disposals of shares. If so, this task is humanly marked and will include a share pool for either an individual or a company, which may include a combination of purchases, disposals, bonus issues and rights issues. The question is likely to be complex with a number of different transactions.

Be careful to remember the matching rules – not all disposals will necessarily be matched with the share pool, therefore it is important to consider these rules first.

The Business Tax reference material provided in your assessment covers the rules for disposals of shares in the sections headed 'Shares and securities – disposals by individuals' and 'Shares and securities – disposals by companies'. The material includes the matching rules and a pro forma for the share pool for company disposals.

62   PUCK LTD

Puck Ltd bought 3,000 shares in Quinn Ltd in June 2008 for £12,000.

In January 2012, there was a 1 for 3 bonus issue and in December 2015 there was a 1 for 4 rights issue at £2 a share.

All shares were sold in April 2020 for £24,000.

Indexation factors were:

	January 2012	December 2015	December 2017	April 2020
June 2008	0.098	0.202		
January 2012		0.095		
December 2015			0.067	0.124

Calculate the chargeable gain on the disposal of these shares using the grid supplied.

63 PISTON LTD

Piston Ltd sold all of its ordinary shares in Power plc for £18,800 on 12 May 2020.

Piston Ltd acquired its shares in Power plc as follows:

10 August 2006	Purchased 2,700 shares for £10,640
19 July 2013	Took up a 1 for 3 bonus issue
20 January 2014	Purchased 2,300 shares for £7,130

Indexation factors were:

August 2006 – July 2013	0.254
August 2006 – January 2014	0.268
July 2013 – January 2014	0.012
January 2014 – December 2017	0.101
January 2014 – May 2020	0.163

Calculate the chargeable gain on the disposal of these shares using the grid supplied.

64   DREAM LTD

Dream Ltd bought 6,000 shares in Boat Ltd for £12,000 in March 2000.

In June 2005 there was a bonus issue of 1 for 2.

In December 2020, 7,000 shares were sold for £46,350.

Indexation factors were:

	June 2005	**December 2017**	**December 2020**
March 2000	0.141	0.651	0.778
June 2005		0.447	0.558

Calculate the chargeable gain on the disposal of these shares using the grid supplied.

65   BATMAN LTD

Batman Ltd bought 7,000 shares in Robin Ltd for £14,000 in May 2006.

It obtained additional shares through a 1 for 8 bonus issue in July 2008 and a 1 for 5 rights issue in July 2012. The rights issue shares were purchased for £3 each.

In September 2020, Batman Ltd sold 5,000 of the shares for £5 per share.

Indexation factors were:

May 2006 to July 2008	0.095
July 2008 to July 2012	0.118
May 2006 to July 2012	0.225
July 2012 to December 2017	0.149
July 2012 to September 2020	0.227

Calculate the chargeable gain on the disposal of these shares using the grid supplied.

66   SHELBYVILLE LTD

On 14 May 2017, Shelbyville Ltd bought 10,000 shares in Springfield plc for £23,300.

On 10 November 2017, Springfield plc issued bonus shares of 1 for 40.

On 29 January 2021, Shelbyville Ltd bought a further 2,000 shares in Springfield plc for £5,950.

On 2 February 2021, Shelbyville Ltd sold 5,875 of these shares for £3.20 each.

Indexation factors were:

May 2017 to November 2017	0.015
November 2017 to January 2021	0.088
November 2017 to February 2021	0.091
May 2017 to December 2017	0.024
May 2017 to January 2021	0.105
May 2017 to February 2021	0.108
January 2021 to February 2021	0.003

Calculate the chargeable gain on the disposal of these shares using the grids supplied.

67   **JAMES**

James bought 1,000 shares in Sian Ltd for £4,500 in July 2010.

A bonus issue of 1 for 10 shares was made in August 2012.

In October 2020, James sold half the shares for £14.20 per share.

Indexation factors were:

	August 2012	**December 2017**	**October 2020**
July 2010	0.087	0.244	0.332
August 2012		0.144	0.226

Calculate the chargeable gain on the disposal of these shares.

68   GOODWIN

Goodwin bought 3,600 shares in Shred Ltd for £25,200 on 11 March 2013.

There was a bonus issue of 1 for 3 shares on 23 July 2014.

Goodwin sold 2,500 shares in Shred Ltd for £9.00 per share on 19 January 2021.

On 4 February 2021 Goodwin purchased a further 800 shares in Shred Ltd for £6,800.

Calculate the chargeable gain on the disposal of the shares on 19 January 2021.

CAPITAL GAINS – RELIEFS

Key answer tips

This section covers a broad range of topics, namely capital gains exemptions, reliefs, losses and the calculation of capital gains tax payable.

Reliefs covered are business asset disposal relief, gift relief and rollover relief – the latter of which is the only relief available to a company. You should also grasp capital losses and be able to calculate the capital gains tax payable by individuals.

The Business Tax reference material provided in your assessment covers these topics in the sections headed 'Introduction to chargeable gains', 'Calculation of gains and losses for individuals', 'Chargeable gains – reliefs available to individuals' and 'Calculation of gains and losses for companies'.

69   SUSAN AND RACHEL

(a)   Which of the following statements is correct?

A   Rollover relief is available to individuals and companies

B   Rollover relief is only available to individuals

C   Rollover relief is only available for a qualifying re-investment within 12 months after disposal

D   Rollover relief is only available to companies

(b)   Susan, aged 60, made a chargeable gain of £550,000 on the sale of her business. She had owned the business for ten years and is now retiring. She is a higher rate taxpayer.

She also realised a gain of £15,000 on the sale of an antique table.

Which of the following statements is not correct?

A   The chargeable gain on the antique table will be taxed at 20%

B   Business asset disposal relief is available on the business gain as all of the conditions have been satisfied

C   The chargeable gain on the business, after the deduction of the annual exempt amount, will be taxed at 10%

D   The annual exempt amount is deducted from the gain on the antique table, leaving all of the business gain to be taxed

(c)   Which of the following statements is correct?

A   Individuals can offset their capital losses against their trading profits in the same tax year

B   Individuals can offset their capital losses against their chargeable gains in the same tax year

C   Individuals can offset their capital losses against their total income in the same tax year

D   Individuals get no relief for their capital losses

(d) Rachel sells an asset to her brother Artie for £15,000 when its market value is £22,000.

Which of the following statements is correct?

A Artie's deemed cost is £7,000

B Rachel's deemed gain is £7,000

C Rachel's deemed proceeds are £15,000

D Rachel's deemed proceeds are £22,000

(e) Varti, a higher rate taxpayer, acquired newly issued shares in Delta Ltd, an unquoted trading company, on 11 April 2016. She has never worked for Delta Ltd. She sold the shares in September 2020 and immediately reinvested the proceeds in shares in Epsilon Ltd.

Which of the following statements is correct?

A Rollover relief is available to defer the gain made on the disposal of the Delta shares

B Varti will be able to claim investors' relief on the disposal of the Delta Ltd shares

C Varti will be able to claim business asset disposal relief on the disposal of the Delta Ltd shares

D The gain made on the disposal of the Delta Ltd shares will be taxed at 20%

70 MALCOLM AND JEREMY

(a) Malcolm bought a warehouse for £350,000 in March 2011.

In June 2020, it was sold for £725,000.

In the same month he bought a factory for £590,000.

What is the amount of the gain that can be rolled over?

Choose from one of the following options:

£240,000; £Nil; £590,000; £375,000; £135,000

(b) Jeremy sold a qualifying business asset on 1 September 2020.

The dates during which the proceeds must be reinvested in another qualifying business asset to be eligible for rollover relief are between:

A	and	B

Choose one date from each of the options below and insert in the appropriate place in the table above.

Options:

A 1 September 2020; 1 September 2017; 6 April 2020; 6 April 2021; 1 September 2019

B 5 April 2021; 5 April 2022; 5 April 2023; 1 September 2019; 1 September 2022; 1 September 2023

71   AVAILABILITY OF RELIEFS

Which one of the following statements is false?

A   Business asset disposal relief is only available to individuals

B   Rollover relief is available to both individuals and companies

C   Gift relief is available to both individuals and companies

D   Investors' relief is not available to companies

72   OLIVER LTD

A factory was sold by Oliver Ltd for £800,000 in May 2020 realising a gain of £300,000.

Which of the following statements is correct in relation to rollover relief?

A   If the company reinvests in a qualifying asset within the qualifying time period then the gain of £300,000 is automatically deferred

B   If the company purchases some shares in an unquoted trading company for £880,000 in November 2020 then it can claim rollover relief

C   If the company purchases a replacement factory for £750,000 in June 2021 then it can use rollover relief to defer £250,000 of the gain

D   If the company purchases a replacement factory for £950,000 in June 2023 then it can use rollover relief to defer the gain

73   JOHN, PAUL, GEORGE AND RINGO

(a)   John sells some unquoted trading company shares in June 2020. He does not work for the company.

The shares are sold for their full market value. Three months later, John reinvests all the proceeds in some more unquoted trading company shares.

Which of the following reliefs are available, if any?

A   Rollover relief

B   Business asset disposal relief

C   Gift relief

D   None of the above

(b)   Paul gives an antique vase to his son for his birthday. It has a market value of £7,000.

Which of the following reliefs are available, if any?

A   Rollover relief

B   Investors' relief

C   Gift relief

D   None of the above

(c)   George sells his 1% interest in unquoted trading company shares to his friend Stuart for £3,000 when their market value is £5,000. The shares cost George £1,000.

Which of the following reliefs are available, if any?

A   Rollover relief

B   Business asset disposal relief

C   Gift relief

D   None of the above

(d)   Ringo sells his stake in a partnership business at its full market value. He had been a partner for three years before the disposal. He does not reinvest any of the sale proceeds.

Which of the following reliefs are available, if any?

A   Rollover relief

B   Business asset disposal relief

C   Gift relief

D   None of the above

74   NORMAN

(a)   Norman has owned 15% of the shares in a trading company since May 2000. He is an employee of the company.

He sells all his shares in December 2020, making a gain before reliefs of £700,000. He has made no other disposals and is a higher rate taxpayer.

What is the capital gains tax payable for 2020/21?

Choose from one of the following options:

£Nil;   £68,770;   £137,540;   £70,000;   £140,000

(b)   What is the deadline for claiming business asset disposal relief for a disposal in 2020/21?

Choose from one of the following options:

31 January 2021;   31 January 2022;   31 January 2023;   31 January 2024;
31 October 2021;   31 October 2022;   31 October 2023;   31 October 2024

75   HARRY AND BRIONY

(a)   Which of the following statements is correct?

A   Shares in an individual's personal trading company are qualifying assets for rollover relief.

B   If only part of the proceeds are reinvested in another qualifying asset, the amount that cannot be rolled over is the higher of the proceeds not reinvested and the chargeable gain.

C   When rollover relief is claimed, the gain is rolled over by adding it to the base cost of the replacement asset.

D   If a qualifying asset is purchased on 1 October 2020 and another is sold on 25 September 2021, the disposal will qualify for rollover relief.

(b)   Harry made a gain qualifying for business asset disposal relief of £300,000 in 2019/20.

A further qualifying gain of £5,500,000 was made in 2020/21.

There were no other disposals in either year and Harry is a higher rate taxpayer.

What is the capital gains tax payable on the gain in 2020/21?

A   £1,027,540

B   £550,000

C   £1,030,000

D   £548,770

(c)   Which of the following statements is correct?

A   Gift relief is only available to companies

B   Gift relief is available to both companies and individuals

C   Gift relief is only available to individuals

(d)   Briony gives an antique vase to her husband, Chris.

Which one of the following statements is correct?

A   Briony's deemed proceeds will be the market value of the vase

B   Briony can claim gift relief for the chargeable gain

C   Briony's chargeable gain will be £Nil

D   Briony's deemed proceeds will be nil so she will have a capital loss

76   CHERYL

    (a)   Which one of the following statements is correct?

        A   A capital loss made by an individual can be carried back against chargeable gains made in the preceding tax year.

        B   A capital loss made by an individual can be carried forward to the following tax year without offsetting it against the current year gains.

        C   A capital loss made by an individual which is brought forward from an earlier year is offset against gains in the tax year but only after deduction of the relevant annual exempt amount for that year.

        D   A capital loss made by an individual can only be carried forward for one tax year.

    (b)   Cheryl gifts an asset to her husband, James.

        The asset originally cost Cheryl £50,000.

        James immediately sells the asset for its market value of £120,000.

        Which one of the following statements is correct?

        A   James has a chargeable gain of nil

        B   Both Cheryl and James's unused annual exempt amounts can be used against the gain

        C   James's deemed cost is £50,000

        D   Cheryl will pay capital gains tax on the gain of £70,000

    (c)   Which one of the following statements is correct?

        A   Business asset disposal relief is available on qualifying business gains of up to £1,000,000 for the lifetime of the taxpayer.

        B   Business asset disposal relief is restricted to £1,000,000 of gains for each disposal of qualifying business assets.

        C   Business asset disposal relief is available for individuals and companies.

        D   Business asset disposal relief is available on the sale of individual business assets.

77   ALLYN AND SIMON

    (a)   Allyn bought a factory for £1,400,000 in January 2014.

        In November 2020, it was sold for £2,850,000.

        In the same month another factory was bought for £2,000,000.

        What is the amount of the gain that can be rolled over?

        Choose from one of the following options:

        £850,000;   £1,450,000;   £600,000;   £1,400,000;   £Nil

(b)   Simon sold a qualifying business asset on 1 February 2019.

The dates during which the proceeds must be reinvested in another qualifying business asset to be eligible for rollover relief are between:

A	and	B

Choose one date from each of the options below and insert in the appropriate place in the table above.

Options:

A   1 February 2018; 1 July 2018; 1 February 2016; 6 April 2018; 5 April 2019

B   1 February 2019; 5 April 2019; 1 February 2020; 6 October 2020;
      1 February 2021; 1 February 2022

78   EVAN, ZAK AND LILIA

Three taxpayers sold investment assets during 2020/21 and each has made a chargeable gain of £120,300. They have not made any other disposals during the tax year. The table below shows their taxable income in 2020/21. The basic rate band in 2020/21 is £37,500.

Complete the amount of gain that would be chargeable under each of the two rates of capital gains tax. You must enter '0' if your answer is zero.

Taxpayer	Taxable income	Chargeable gain	
		10% CGT	20% CGT
	£	£	£
Evan	21,500		
Zak	29,700		
Lilia	42,300		

79   OPHELIA, GEORGIA AND SID

Three taxpayers sold pieces of land and each has made a taxable gain of £14,000 after deduction of the annual exempt amount. They have not made any other disposals during the tax year. The table below shows their taxable income in 2020/21. The basic rate band in 2020/21 is £37,500.

Complete the amount of gain that would be chargeable under each of the two rates of capital gains tax. You must enter '0' if your answer is zero.

Taxpayer	Taxable income	Chargeable gain	
		10% CGT	20% CGT
	£	£	£
Ophelia	38,000		
Georgia	24,200		
Sid	19,850		

NATIONAL INSURANCE CONTRIBUTIONS

SELF-EMPLOYED INDIVIDUALS

Key answer tips

Only classes 2 and 4 are assessable; however, you may be asked to calculate the NICs payable by sole traders or partners.

The Business Tax reference material provided in your assessment covers this topic in the section headed 'National insurance contributions'.

---

80   JENNY AND JACK

    (a)   Jenny has self-employed income of £85,000 for 2020/21.

           The amount of class 4 NICs payable (to the nearest pence) is: £ [   ]

    (b)   Jack has self-employed income of £25,000 for 2020/21.

           The amount of class 2 NICs payable (to the nearest pence) is: £ [   ]

    (c)   Which of the following statements is correct?

        A   Self-employed taxpayers pay class 4 NICs based on the drawings taken out of the business

        B   Self-employed taxpayers pay NICs based on the salary they pay to themselves

        C   Self-employed taxpayers can pay both class 2 and class 4 NICs

        D   Self-employed taxpayers only pay NICs for their employees and not for themselves

81 CARTER

Carter, who has been trading for many years, draws up accounts to 31 December each year.

The results of the business are as follows:

	Accounting profit £	Taxable profit £
Year ended 31 December 2020	8,500	6,600
Year ended 31 December 2021	7,678	2,500

Which of the following statements is correct?

A   Carter is liable to both class 2 and class 4 NICs for 2020/21

B   Carter is liable to neither class 2 nor class 4 NICs for 2020/21

C   Carter is liable to class 2, but not class 4 NICs for 2020/21

D   Carter is liable to class 4, but not class 2 NICs for 2020/21

82 IVOR

(a)   Ivor's share of his partnership's taxable trading income is £100,000 for 2020/21.

      The amount chargeable to class 4 NICs at 9% is: £ _____

(b)   The amount chargeable to class 4 NICs at 2% is: £ _____

(c)   The amount of class 2 NICs payable (to the nearest pence) is: £ _____

(d)   Tick the appropriate box.

	True	False
Ivor will also be required to pay class 1 primary NICs in relation to his salary from the partnership		

83 JAKE, SUE AND PETE

(a)   Jake's sole trader business has made a taxable trading profit of £60,000 for 2020/21.

      The amount of class 2 NICs payable by Jake (to the nearest pence) for the year is: £ _____

(b)   Sue has taxable trading profits of £41,000 for 2020/21.

      The amount of total class 4 NICs payable by Sue (to the nearest pence) is: £ _____

(c)   Pete's sole trader business has made a taxable trading profit of £4,000 for 2020/21.

      The total amount of NICs payable by Pete (to the nearest pence) is: £ _____

84   THOMAS AND SUZANNE

(a)   Thomas received a state pension of £6,980 throughout 2020/21 and had self-employed income of £55,000 for 2020/21.

The amount chargeable to class 4 NICs at 9% is:

£ _____

(b)   Suzanne, aged 42, has self-employed income of £35,000 for 2020/21.

The amount of total class 4 NICs payable (to the nearest pence) is:

£ _____

(c)   Which of the following statements is correct?

A   Every self-employed taxpayer must pay class 2 NICs, irrespective of the level of profits

B   Self-employed taxpayers pay both class 2 and class 4, never just one of them

C   Class 4 NICs are based on the accounting profits of the business

D   In a partnership, each partner is responsible for his/her own NICs

85   AMELIE AND ALEXANDER

Amelie and Alexander are in partnership sharing profits in the ratio 60:40 after paying a salary of £5,000 to Alexander. The partnership's taxable trading profit for the year ended 31 March 2021 was £75,000.

(a)   The amount of class 4 NICs payable by Amelie (to the nearest pence) is:

£ _____

(b)   The amount of class 4 NICs payable by Alexander (to the nearest pence) is:

£ _____

(c)   The amount of class 2 NICs payable by Amelie (to the nearest pence) is:

£ _____

CURRENT TAX RELIEFS AND OTHER TAX ISSUES

R&D TAX CREDITS AND IR35

Key answer tips

The Business Tax reference material provided in your assessment covers two topics here – Research and development tax credits and Intermediaries (IR35) legislation.

86 BARRY

Barry wishes you to tell him which of the following statements are true and which false.

Tick the appropriate box for each statement.

	True	False
Ellis plc is an SME. It has already deducted £40,000 of qualifying research and development cost from its profits. It can deduct a further £92,000 in arriving at its adjusted trading profit.		
Jade plc has annual turnover below 100 million euros. It is automatically classed as an SME.		
The cost of heating and lighting a research and development department can never be part of the qualifying cost for R&D tax credits.		

87 CAITLIN

Caitlin wishes you to tell her which of the following statements are true and which false.

Tick the appropriate box for each statement.

	True	False
Employers' NIC for staff involved in research and development activities can be part of the qualifying cost for R&D tax credits.		
If an SME makes a loss due to qualifying research and development expenditure it must surrender the loss in return for a cash payment.		
Capital expenditure of £50,000 is incurred by an SME on qualifying research and development projects. The company can claim capital allowances on £115,000 (£50,000 × 230%).		

88 JOE

Joe wishes you to tell him which of the following statements are true and which false.

Tick the appropriate box for each statement.

	True	False
All the turnover of a personal service company (PSC) is automatically subject to a deemed employment income tax charge.		
IR35 legislation exists to prevent a PSC from being used to disguise permanent employment.		
If a PSC has only one client it is an indication that this is a disguised employment.		
If a PSC has several clients then none of its income will be subject to an employment income charge.		

89   IRIS

Iris wishes you to tell her which of the following statements are true and which false.

Tick the appropriate box for each statement.

	True	False
Central plc engages Zoom Ltd to provide some consultancy services. Zoom Ltd is a PSC. If the contract between Central plc and Zoom Ltd is deemed to be a relevant engagement under IR35 rules then Central plc must deduct income tax and NIC from the payments made to Zoom Ltd.		
If the owner of a PSC provides his/her own tools and equipment in carrying out a contract for a client then that contract cannot be deemed to be a relevant engagement subject to IR35 rules.		
If the owner of a PSC cannot send a substitute to carry out work for a client but must perform the work himself/herself, then that is an indication that the contract may be deemed to be a relevant engagement subject to IR35 rules.		

SELF-ASSESSMENT

Key answer tips

Self-assessment rules and ethics are important areas and can be tested with a written style task or smaller multi-part questions. The task could include questions on the rules relating to payments of tax (including the calculation of payments on account), filing of returns and penalties, as well as the ethics of confidentiality and communication with HMRC.

Payment dates for companies are also covered in this section.

The Business Tax reference material provided in your assessment covers these topics in the sections headed 'Payment and administration – sole traders and partners', 'Enquiries and other penalties', 'Corporation tax – payment and administration' and 'Duties and responsibilities of a tax adviser'.

PAYMENT DATES

90   INDIVIDUAL'S PAYMENT DATES

State when the following are due:

(a)   First instalment of income tax for tax year 2020/21:

(b)   Final payment of income tax for tax year 2020/21:

(c)   Capital gains tax payable for tax year 2020/21:

(d)   Second instalment of class 4 NICs for tax year 2020/21:

91 PAYMENTS ON ACCOUNT (POAs)

Tick the appropriate box for each statement.

	True	False
POAs are not required if the income tax and class 4 NIC payable for the previous year by self-assessment is less than £1,000		
POAs for 2020/21 are due on 31 July 2021 and 31 January 2022		
POAs are not required if more than 80% of the income tax and capital gains tax liability for the previous year was met through tax deducted under PAYE		
POAs of class 2 NICs are never required		
POAs of class 4 NICs are optional; the taxpayer can choose to pay under monthly direct debit or quarterly invoice if they prefer		

92 COMPANY PAYMENT DATES

What is the first payday for corporation tax for a company with augmented profits of £800,000, assuming:

(a) a 12 month period ended 31 March 2021, a shareholding of 51% in a group company and where the company had similar results in the previous year:

(b) a nine month period ending 31 December 2020 and no 51% group companies:

(c) a 12 month period ended 31 January 2021 and no 51% group companies:

(d) a seven month period ended 31 October 2021, a shareholding of 51% in a group company and was a large company in previous years:

93 DUE DATES

For each of the following statements, fill in the blanks:

(a) An individual pays the second instalment of income tax under self-assessment for 2020/21 on ....

(b) An individual must file a paper income tax return for 2020/21 by ....

(c) A company with augmented profits of £400,000 for the year ended 31 December 2020 must pay its corporation tax by ....

(d) A .... company pays by instalments based on the .... year's profits

94   COMPANY DUE DATES

A company has prepared its accounts for the year ended 31 March 2021.

For the following, state when each are due:

(a)   Submission of the corporation tax return:

(b)   Payment of corporation tax liability, assuming augmented profits are below £1,500,000:

(c)   First instalment of corporation tax liability, assuming the company is required to pay by quarterly instalments:

(d)   Final instalment of corporation tax liability, assuming the company is required to pay by quarterly instalments:

ADMINISTRATION, PENALTIES AND ETHICAL STANDARDS

95   IRFAN

Irfan asks whether the following statements are true or false.

Tick the appropriate box for each statement.

	True	False
An individual must retain tax records for his/her business for 2020/21 until 5 April 2023		
If an individual is seven months late in submitting the tax return for 2020/21, he/she will receive a maximum penalty of £200		
The maximum penalty for a mistake in a tax return due to carelessness is 70%		
If an individual's balancing payment for 2020/21 is two months late he/she can be charged a late payment penalty of 5%		
A company with a period of account ending 30 September 2020 must submit its tax return by 30 September 2021		
Interest is charged on late payments of balancing payments and instalments		

96   COMPLIANCE CHECKS AND APPEALS

(a)   Jane submitted her 2019/20 tax return on 13 January 2021.

By what date must HMRC give notice if they wish to commence a compliance check?

A   31 January 2021

B   31 January 2022

C   13 January 2022

D   30 April 2022

(b)   Jane asks whether the following statements are true or false.

Tick the appropriate box for each statement.

	True	False
A closed compliance check can be reopened within 9 months of the completion notice		
The taxpayer's right of appeal against an amended assessment on the closure of a compliance check must be made within 30 days of the completion notice		
Where a company has submitted its tax return on time, the deadline for HMRC to commence a compliance check is two years after the end of the company's accounting period		
In complex tax cases HMRC can close discrete matters in a compliance check, whilst other issues remain open		

(c)   Where the Upper Tier of the Tax Tribunal have determined an appeal on a point of law and the taxpayer expresses dissatisfaction, the case will then be referred to:

A   the Court of Appeal and then the Supreme Court (if necessary)

B   No one – there is only a right of appeal based on fact

C   the European Court of Justice

D   the Treasury

97   NAGINA

Nagina asks whether the following statements are true or false.

Tick the appropriate box for each statement.

	True	False
The maximum penalty for failing to keep records is £3,000 per accounting period		
The maximum penalty for a failure to notify chargeability is 100% of the tax due but unpaid		
A late payment penalty can apply to payments on account of income tax		
Companies can choose whether to file paper tax returns or file online		

98   PENALTIES

(a)   What is the maximum penalty for submitting a corporation tax return more than six but less than 12 months late?

    A   £100

    B   £200 plus 10% of the tax due

    C   £200

    D   £200 plus 20% of the tax due

(b)   What is the maximum penalty for deliberate understatement without concealment in a tax return?

    A   £100

    B   10% of tax unpaid

    C   70% of tax unpaid

    D   100% of tax unpaid

(c)   What is the penalty for a company's failure to keep records for six years?

    A   Up to £3,000 for each accounting period affected

    B   Up to £6,000 for each accounting period affected

    C   Up to £3,000 in total

    D   Up to £6,000 in total

(d)   What is the penalty for late filing of an income tax return if it is less than three months late?

    A   £100

    B   £200

    C   £300

    D   10% of tax unpaid

99 MANINDER

Maninder asks whether the following statements are true or false.

Tick the appropriate box for each statement.

	True	False
The filing deadline for electronic submission of an individual's 2020/21 tax return is 31 January 2022		
A self-employed individual is required to keep records to support his/her 2020/21 tax return until 31 January 2027		
There is no penalty for late submission of an individual's tax return as long as it is less than six months late		
If a company makes a mistake in the tax return due to failure to take reasonable care, there is a penalty of up to 30%		
An individual should make the first payment on account for 2020/21 on 31 January 2022		

100 JANET

Janet asks whether the following statements are true or false.

Tick the appropriate box for each statement.

	True	False
If an individual is eight months late in submitting the tax return for 2020/21, he/she will receive a penalty of £200		
The maximum penalties for errors made by individuals in their tax returns vary from 20% to 100%		
If a company fails to keep records for the appropriate period of time, it can be fined up to £2,000		
A company with a period of account ending on 30 June 2020, must keep its records until 30 June 2028		
Late payment penalties are not normally imposed on payments on account		

101 ETHICAL RULES (1)

(a) Which ONE of the following statements is not correct?

   A   Accountants must not associate themselves with returns which contain false or misleading statements

   B   Accountants should not be associated with returns which contain information provided recklessly without any real knowledge of whether they are true or false

   C   Accountants are allowed to be associated with returns which may omit information which would mislead HMRC

   D   Accountants must not be associated with returns which obscure information in a way which would mislead HMRC

(b)   When an accountant is giving a client advice, with whom can he/she share the information? Choose one option.

A   HMRC

B   Other clients with identical circumstances

C   The client

102   ETHICAL RULES (2)

(a)   Which ONE of the following statements is not correct?

A   Accountants should not be involved with tax returns that omit information

B   Accountants should not be associated with a return that contains misleading information

C   Accountants who are involved with returns that deliberately contain false information can be subject to a penalty

D   Accountants should never prepare tax returns for clients

(b)   When can an accountant divulge confidential information?

A   If the information is over six years old

B   If a member of the public asks for it

C   If the accountant has written authority from the client to disclose

D   If the client's spouse requests the information

103   CLIENT ADVICE

(a)   Which ONE of the following statements is not correct?

A   Accountants need to follow the rules of confidentiality unless given permission by a client

B   Accountants can break the rules of confidentiality when the public interest is threatened

C   Tax evasion is a legal means of reducing your tax liability

D   The AAT expects its members to maintain an objective outlook

(b)   When an accountant is advising a client, to whom does he/she owe the greatest duty of care?

A   The accountant's employer

B   The AAT

C   The client

D   The government

104 AAT STUDENT

(a)   Which of the following statements is not correct?

A   As a student of the AAT you are bound by the duty of confidentiality

B   The rules of confidentiality do not need to be followed when a wife asks for information about her husband's tax matters

C   The rules of confidentiality need to be followed even after the client relationship has ended

D   Confidentiality means not disclosing information you acquire due to your job

(b)   When an accountant is working for a client, when can the rules of confidentiality be breached?

A   If the accountant does not agree with what the client is saying

B   If the client refuses to correct an error in his/her tax return

C   If the accountant resigns

D   If the client is suspected of money laundering

105 NASHEEN

Nasheen is a student member of the AAT. She asks whether the following statements are true or false.

Tick the appropriate box for each statement.

	True	False
If a husband is ill, it is acceptable to discuss his tax affairs with his wife even if no letter of authorisation exists.		
Accountants must follow the rules of confidentiality irrespective of the situation.		

106 TAX RETURN RESPONSIBILITY

Who is ultimately responsible for ensuring that a taxpayer's tax return is accurately completed?

A   HMRC

B   Tax adviser

C   Taxpayer

D   HM Treasury

107 LAREDO

Laredo asks whether the following statements are true or false.

Tick the appropriate box for each statement.

	True	False
All business tax records for an individual should be kept for at least four years.		
The maximum penalty for not keeping records is £2,000.		
An individual whose income tax and class 4 NIC payable by self-assessment for the previous tax year is less than £1,000 is not required to make payments on account.		
Tax on chargeable gains is paid in two instalments on 31 January in the tax year and 31 July following the end of the tax year.		

WRITTEN QUESTIONS

108 MALIK

Malik has written to you with the following query:

> Further to our earlier conversation, I am writing with a query about national insurance. As you know, I have a small amount of investment income and in June 2020 I started my own business selling hand-made children's toys and made a taxable profit of £1,200 for the year ended 31 December 2020. I only paid income tax of £850 for the tax year 2020/21. I paid no national insurance, on your advice. The good news is that I have just been awarded a large contract which will increase my taxable profits significantly for the year ended 31 December 2021. I am still in negotiations at the moment so am not sure of the exact value of the contract, but I hope it will be at least £15,000.
>
> Thanks for explaining the payments on account system for income tax, but can you explain what national insurance contributions I will have to pay as a result of the new contract.
>
> Many thanks

You are required to respond appropriately to Malik's query.

109 BAMBOO LTD

The finance director of Bamboo Ltd has written to your manager with the following query:

> We have a few issues with regard to our tax returns within the group, so can I ask you two questions please?
>
> The financial controller of Ash Ltd has told me that there is an error on the spread sheet that he used to report the rental income for this company for the year ended 30 June 2019 and the rent is understated by £16,000. This is apparently due to a bug in the computer file. He contacted HMRC within a week of discovering the issue and they seem to agree it is a mistake, but what penalty can I expect as a result of this problem?
>
> I have just been told that the corporation tax return for Elm Ltd for the year ended 30 June 2019 was not filed until 7 June 2020, despite my instructions that all returns for all companies in the group should be filed by 1 June 2020. Can you explain any penalties we will incur as a result of this?
>
> Many thanks for your help.

You are required to draft a reply to respond appropriately to this query.

110 SARA

> Your manager has forwarded the following email to you from one of your firm's clients, Sara, who is self-employed.
>
> I received a letter from HMRC yesterday telling me that they are going to commence a compliance check on my 2019/20 income tax return, which I filed six months ago. Surely they should have told me earlier? Can you let me know what will happen as a result of this compliance check (should I send them documents?) and what action I can take if I disagree with the findings.

Draft an appropriate response to be passed to your manager.

111 CHARLIE

Charlie has written to you with the following query:

> 'I am writing to you for some clarification on my tax liabilities. Although I have been paying tax for a long time I still do not understand what needs paying and when.
>
> My tax payable was £8,600 for 2019/20. According to your calculation I will owe £9,000 for 2020/21.
>
> Could you please explain to me how my payments are calculated, and what they should have been for 2020/21 so I can check the HMRC figures.
>
> Many thanks for your time.
>
> Charlie

You need to respond appropriately to his query.

112 MELANIE

> Your manager has forwarded the following email to you from Melanie. Melanie is an investment banker and a client of your firm.
>
> 'I inherited a number of items of furniture following the death of my father. I renovated the furniture, kept some of the items and sold the rest for a total of £4,000. I know that the items of furniture are exempt for the purposes of capital gains tax, but I am not sure of my position in relation to income tax. Also, I enjoyed the renovation work so much that I am considering purchasing more furniture, which I will then restore and sell at a profit.'

Your manager has provided you with a list of the factors, known as the badges of trade, which will be considered by HM Revenue and Customs in determining whether or not Melanie's activities will be regarded as the carrying on of a trade.

In relation to four of these factors only, explain whether you think Melanie will be treated as carrying on a trade.

113 CHARLOTTE

Charlotte is a new client who has been building up her sole trader business since her retirement in 2016. She has written to you with the following query dated 1 November 2021.

'I wonder if you could explain a few things for me about tax payments. My previous accountants gave me the following information for 2020/21:

	£
Income tax liability	14,580
Less: Tax deducted at source	(5,250)
	9,330
Capital gains tax liability	4,900
Tax payable	14,230

I never used to pay any tax by instalments but I paid £4,000 tax on 31 January 2021 and again on 31 July 2021. I don't understand how much I will have to pay on 31 January 2022.

Please can you tell me how much I will have to pay by that date and what happens if I pay my tax late.

I am sure you remember that I don't pay national insurance any more as I am receiving my state pension.'

You need to respond appropriately to her query.

114 SOPHIA

You have received the following e-mail from Sophia dated 14 September 2021.

I am a bit worried as I have been receiving interest from a loan to my brother but have never told you about it because I thought it was a private arrangement and not taxable. However my brother says I should have included it on my tax return.

He first started paying me interest in June 2019 so I suppose it should have been included on my 2019/20 tax return. As you are still working on my 2020/21 return it will not be a problem to alter that.

Please advise what we should do now and the consequences of this mistake. The interest was £1,500 in 2019/20 and £1,800 in 2020/21.

You should reply to Sophia's email. Sophia is a higher rate taxpayer.

TAX RETURNS

Key answer tips

The two tax returns which can be tested are sections from the self-employed return and the partnership return.

It is vital that you are careful to complete the correct boxes on the return – it is not enough to just enter the right numbers somewhere! Care and attention to detail are crucial to score full marks in this task.

115 JORDAN

Complete the return below as far as is possible using the following information.

Boxes 17 to 31 have already been completed.

Included in the expenses listed in Jordan's personal income tax return, the following information is relevant:

1   Irrecoverable debts written off comprise:

	£
Increase in specific irrecoverable debt provision	800
Increase in general irrecoverable debt provision	268
Trade debts written off	672
Trade debts recovered	(200)

2   Rent, rates and insurance include:

	£
Expenses relating to the flat where the owner lives	3,000

3   Motor expenses include:

	£
Van expenses (van used by owner exclusively for the business)	5,090
Car expenses (car used by owner exclusively for private purposes)	2,690

4   Wages and salaries include:

	£
Owner's drawings	18,000

5   Miscellaneous expenses include:

	£
Gifts of diaries to customers	800
– costing £8 each and bearing the logo of the business	
Parking fines incurred by owner	280

Business expenses

Please read the 'Self-employment (full) notes' before filling in this section.

Total expenses	Disallowable expenses
If your annual turnover was below £85,000, you may just put your total expenses in box 31	Use this column if the figures in boxes 17 to 30 include disallowable amounts

17 Cost of goods bought for resale or goods used

£ 2 0 8 1 7 8 · 0 0

32 £ · 0 0

18 Construction industry – payments to subcontractors

£ · 0 0

33 £ · 0 0

19 Wages, salaries and other staff costs

£ 3 5 6 0 4 · 0 0

34 £ · 0 0

20 Car, van and travel expenses

£ 1 3 1 1 2 · 0 0

35 £ · 0 0

21 Rent, rates, power and insurance costs

£ 1 4 2 4 0 · 0 0

36 £ · 0 0

22 Repairs and maintenance of property and equipment

£ 3 4 0 · 0 0

37 £ · 0 0

23 Phone, fax, stationery and other office costs

£ 7 4 2 · 0 0

38 £ · 0 0

24 Advertising and business entertainment costs

£ · 0 0

39 £ · 0 0

25 Interest on bank and other loans

£ · 0 0

40 £ · 0 0

26 Bank, credit card and other financial charges

£ · 0 0

41 £ · 0 0

27 Irrecoverable debts written off

£ 1 5 4 0 · 0 0

42 £ · 0 0

28 Accountancy, legal and other professional fees

£ 9 8 0 · 0 0

43 £ · 0 0

29 Depreciation and loss/profit on sale of assets

£ 6 1 4 4 · 0 0

44 £ · 0 0

30 Other business expenses

£ 1 7 7 8 · 0 0

45 £ · 0 0

31 Total expenses (total of boxes 17 to 30)

£ 2 8 2 6 5 8 · 0 0

46 Total disallowable expenses (total of boxes 32 to 45)

£ · 0 0

Adapted from SA103F 2020, page 2, HMRC

116   BINTOU

Complete the return below as far as is possible using the following information.

Boxes 17 to 31 have already been completed.

Included in the expenses listed in Bintou's personal income tax return, the following information is relevant:

1   Bintou has taken drawings of £3,000. This is included in salaries expense.

2   Advertising and entertaining includes:

	£
Gifts to customers:	
Bottles of wine costing £10 each	1,500
Electronic diaries carrying the business's logo, costing £70 each	210
Staff Christmas party for 20 employees	2,000
Client entertaining	600

3   Motor expenses include:

	£
Sales manager's car	6,915
Bintou's car (60% private usage)	2,400

4   Rent, rates and power include:

	£
Electricity for Bintou's house (which is not used in the business)	4,000

Business expenses

Please read the 'Self-employment (full) notes' before filling in this section.

Total expenses

If your annual turnover was below £85,000, you may just put your total expenses in box 31

17	Cost of goods bought for resale or goods used
	£ 1 0 8 1 9 5 · 0 0

18	Construction industry – payments to subcontractors
	£ · 0 0

19	Wages, salaries and other staff costs
	£ 6 5 6 5 0 · 0 0

20	Car, van and travel expenses
	£ 1 0 1 1 0 · 0 0

21	Rent, rates, power and insurance costs
	£ 1 2 2 5 0 · 0 0

22	Repairs and maintenance of property and equipment
	£ · 0 0

23	Phone, fax, stationery and other office costs
	£ 2 7 5 5 · 0 0

24	Advertising and business entertainment costs
	£ 8 6 6 5 · 0 0

25	Interest on bank and other loans
	£ · 0 0

26	Bank, credit card and other financial charges
	£ · 0 0

27	Irrecoverable debts written off
	£ 5 1 0 · 0 0

28	Accountancy, legal and other professional fees
	£ 2 9 8 0 · 0 0

29	Depreciation and loss/profit on sale of assets
	£ 1 6 1 4 0 · 0 0

30	Other business expenses
	£ 1 7 6 0 · 0 0

31	Total expenses (total of boxes 17 to 30)
	£ 2 2 9 0 1 5 · 0 0

Disallowable expenses

Use this column if the figures in boxes 17 to 30 include disallowable amounts

32	£ · 0 0
33	£ · 0 0
34	£ · 0 0
35	£ · 0 0
36	£ · 0 0
37	£ · 0 0
38	£ · 0 0
39	£ · 0 0
40	£ · 0 0
41	£ · 0 0
42	£ · 0 0
43	£ · 0 0
44	£ · 0 0
45	£ · 0 0

46	Total disallowable expenses (total of boxes 32 to 45)
	£ · 0 0

Adapted from SA103F 2020, page 2, HMRC

117 LYNNE AND SHIRLEY PETERS

Complete the return below for the partnership as a whole and for Lynne Peters using the following information.

Lynne and Shirley Peters have traded in partnership for many years as social event organisers, sharing profits 3:2.

Their tax adjusted trading profits for the year ended 31 March 2021 are £230,400, and the partnership received bank interest of £6,210.

Partnership Statement (short) for the year ended 5 April 2021

Please read these instructions before completing the Statement

Use these pages to allocate partnership income if the only income for the relevant return period was trading and professional income or untaxed interest and alternative finance receipts from UK banks and building societies. Otherwise you must download the 'Partnership Statement (Full)' pages to record details of the allocation of all the partnership income. Go to www.gov.uk/taxreturnforms

Step 1   Fill in boxes 1 to 29 and boxes A and B as appropriate. Get the figures you need from the relevant boxes in the Partnership Tax Return. Complete a separate Statement for each accounting period covered by this Partnership Tax Return and for each trade or profession carried on by the partnership.

Step 2   Then allocate the amounts in boxes 11 to 29 attributable to each partner using the allocation columns on this page and page 7, read the Partnership Tax Return Guide, go to www.gov.uk/taxreturnforms
If the partnership has more than 3 partners, please photocopy page 7.

Step 3   Each partner will need a copy of their allocation of income to fill in their personal tax return.

PARTNERSHIP INFORMATION

If the partnership business includes a trade or profession, enter here the accounting period for which appropriate items in this statement are returned.

Start	1	/ /
End	2	/ /
Nature of trade	3	

Individual partner details

6   Name of partner

Address

Postcode

MIXED PARTNERSHIPS

Tick here if this Statement is drawn up using Corporation Tax rules   **4**

Tick here if this Statement is drawn up using tax rules for non-residents   **5**

Date appointed as a partner
(if during 2019–20 or 2020–21)

Partner's Unique Taxpayer Reference (UTR)

7	/ /	8	

Date ceased to be a partner
(if during 2019–20 or 2020–21)

Partner's National Insurance number

9	/ /	10	

Partnership's profits, losses, income and tax credits

Tick this box if the items entered in the box had foreign tax taken off

Partner's share of profits, losses, income and tax credits

Copy figures in boxes 11 to 29 to boxes in the individual's Partnership (short) pages as shown below

- for an accounting period ended in 2020-21 ▼

from box 3.83	Profit from a trade or profession	**A**	**11** £	Profit	**11** £	Copy this figure to box 8
from box 3.82	Adjustment on change of basis		**11A** £		**11A** £	Copy this figure to box 10
from box 3.84	Loss from a trade or profession	**B**	**12** £	Loss	**12** £	Copy this figure to box 8
from box 3.94	Disguised remuneration		**12A**		**12A**	Copy to box 15

- for the period 6 April 2020 to 5 April 2021*

from box 7.9A	Income from untaxed UK savings	**13** £		**13** £	Copy this figure to box 28
from box 3.97	CIS deductions made by contractors on account of tax	**24** £		**24** £	Copy this figure to box 30
from box 3.98	Other tax taken off trading income	**24A** £		**24A** £	Copy this figure to box 31
from box 3.117	Partnership charges	**29** £		**29** £	Copy this figure to box 4, 'Other tax reliefs' section on page Ai 2 in your personal tax return

* If you're a 'CT Partnership' see the Partnership Tax Return Guide

Adapted from SA800 2020, HMRC

Section 2

ANSWERS TO PRACTICE QUESTIONS

INCOME TAX AND CORPORATION TAX

CAPITAL AND REVENUE EXPENDITURE

1 GILES

	Revenue	Capital
Decorating an office	✓	
Computer for a salesman		✓
Office building extension		✓
Electricity for the quarter to 31 March 2021	✓	
Meal to entertain a customer from Germany	✓	
Fork lift truck for the warehouse		✓

2 PHILIP

	Revenue	Capital
Printer for the office computer		✓
Water rates	✓	
Legal fees for purchase of a building		✓

Tutorial note

Costs relating to the purchase of a capital asset will be included as part of its capital cost. Hence the legal fees incurred on purchase of the building should be debited to capital not revenue expenses. For tax purposes legal fees related to a capital acquisition are always treated as capital expenditure and disallowed in the computation of adjusted profits.

3 BROWN

	Revenue	Capital
Repairs to a boiler	✓	
Insurance for motor cars	✓	
Replacement of a severely damaged roof on a newly-purchased warehouse before being able to use the building		✓
Parking fine incurred by Brown	✓	

Tutorial note

1   *Expenditure to repair a newly acquired asset is normally treated as revenue expenditure if the asset is in a serviceable condition when purchased.*

However, where the asset cannot be used in the business unless further expenditure is incurred on it, and the purchase price reflects the state of disrepair, any subsequent repair expenditure is treated as part of the original capital cost of purchase of the asset.

2   *The parking fine of the owner is a revenue expense and will be deducted in the statement of profit or loss of the business.*

It is not a tax allowable expense; however this question does not require you to consider that aspect.

4 BADGES OF TRADE

	Carrying on a trade	Not carrying on a trade
Fred buys a painting in 2013 for £40,000 and hangs it in his home. In 2020 he sells the painting for £50,000 as he needs the cash to pay for a new house.		✓
Franz regularly buys items in charity shops and then sells them soon after on online auction sites for a higher price. He estimates that each week he has a cash profit of £250 from the sales.	✓	
Each month Jason buys an old car and then repairs it prior to selling it at a profit. He has rented a lock up garage to carry out this work. He uses the money he receives from selling a car to buy the next car.	✓	

Tutorial note

In order to decide if an individual is trading it is often useful to look at the 'badges of trade'. These are tests which were originally developed by a Royal Commission in the 1950s and have been further developed by case law over the years.

The badges of trade are:

– *Profit seeking motive*

– *Number of transactions*

– *Nature of asset*

– *Existence of similar trading transactions or interests*

– *Changes to the asset*

– *The way the sale was carried out*

– *The source of finance*

– *Interval of time between purchase and sale*

– *Method of acquisition*

These are listed in the Business Tax reference material provided in your assessment in the section headed 'The badges of trade'.

Applying these tests to the above situations:

Fred bought a painting to enjoy at home. He has sold only one painting in a seven year period. This is not frequent. He has been forced to sell to raise cash and he will not be considered to be trading.

Franz has regular transactions, buying items specifically to sell and not for personal enjoyment. He does not keep the items for a long time. He makes a profit and is likely to be considered as trading.

Jason frequently buys and sells cars. He undertakes supplementary work on the cars and has hired premises to carry out the work. He finances the purchase of the cars with the profits from previous cars. He is likely to be considered to be trading.

ADJUSTMENT OF PROFITS

Key answer tips

The chief assessor has commented in the past that when learners have failed in this type of task, it seems to be due to lack of robust knowledge on areas such as lease payments, adjustments for private use by the owner of the business and what is capital and what is not. A common error would be to adjust for the business use element of the expenses as opposed to adjusting for the private element.

5 FINN

Tax adjusted trading profit computation – year ended 31 March 2021

	£	£
Net profit		107,270
Wages and salaries	0	
Rent and rates	0	
Repairs	10,000	
Advertising and entertaining	1,050	
Accountancy and legal costs	0	
Motor expenses (50% × £6,000)	3,000	
Leasing costs (15% × £8,000)	1,200	
Telephone and office costs	0	
Depreciation	26,525	
Other expenses (£500 + £400)	900	
	———	42,675
		———
		149,945
Capital allowances		(21,070)
		———
Adjusted net profit		128,875
		———

Tutorial note

1   *Gifts to customers costing less than £50 per person per year and carrying a conspicuous advertisement for the business are tax allowable. However, gifts of food, drink, tobacco and vouchers are not allowable.*

2   *15% of the leasing costs for high emission cars (CO_2 emissions over 110g/km) are disallowed.*

3   *The donation to Children in Need is a donation to a national charity and is not allowable in the adjustment of profits computation. Provided the donation is made under the gift aid rules, tax relief is available for the donation in Finn's personal income tax computation. The operation of this relief is covered in personal tax.*

6 FLUSH LTD

	Allowable	Disallowable	CAs available
Decorating an office	✓		
Computer for a salesman		✓	✓
Office building extension		✓	
Electricity for the quarter to 31 March 2021	✓		
Fork lift truck for the warehouse		✓	✓
Meal to entertain a customer from Italy		✓	
Printer for the office computer		✓	✓
Interest payable on a loan to purchase an investment property		✓	
Dividends payable		✓	
Costs of a fraud carried out by a director. These costs are not covered by insurance.		✓	

Tutorial note

There are no capital allowances available on office buildings.

Entertaining customers (UK or overseas) is not allowable.

Interest on loans for a non-trading purpose, such as buying an investment, is disallowed in the adjusted profit computation but is allowed as a deduction from non-trading interest received.

Note that despite the loan being in relation to an investment property, for companies the interest is not deducted against property income. All interest payable for non-trading purposes is deducted from interest income.

Dividends are appropriations of profit and not allowable as an expense.

The costs of a fraud carried out by directors are not allowable. If the fraud had been carried out by an employee the costs would have been allowed.

7 JAMIE

Tax adjusted trading profit computation – year ended 31 March 2021

	£	£
Net loss		(22,066)
Add: Depreciation	40,355	
Jamie's salary	28,000	
Jamie's wife's salary	12,500	
Jamie's motorbike (30% × £2,250)	675	
Entertaining customers	625	
Caviar (2 × £150)	300	
	–––––	82,455
		–––––
		60,389
Less: Capital allowances		(42,236)
		–––––
Tax adjusted trading profit		18,153
		–––––

Tutorial note

1   Salaries paid to family members are allowable provided they represent reasonable remuneration for the services provided to the business. As Jamie's wife does not work for the business at all, none of that expense is allowable. It is assumed, however, that the salary paid to his daughter for her role as Financial Controller of the business is reasonable remuneration.

2   Entertaining staff is allowable for the business, irrespective of the amount spent. Any other form of entertaining is not allowable.

3   Gifts to customers costing less than £50 per person per year and carrying a conspicuous advertisement for the business are tax allowable. Therefore the recipe book expenditure will be allowable.

4   Where the owner takes goods out of the business, for tax purposes, it is treated as a sale to himself at full market value. Jamie must therefore account for the profit element of the transaction (£200 – £50 = £150 per tin of caviar) in his adjustment of profit computation.

8   CRUSH LTD

	Allowable	Disallowable	CAs available
Water rates	✓		
Building insurance	✓		
Replacement of factory machinery		✓	✓
Replacement of a severely damaged roof on an office building	✓		
Insurance for motor cars	✓		
Parking fine incurred by an employee	✓		

Tutorial note

1   Replacement of the whole of an asset such as the factory machinery is a capital item. The replacement of part of an asset, such as the damaged roof of the office building will be treated as revenue expenditure.

2   Parking fines incurred by non-senior employees whilst on business activity are allowable for tax purposes.

9   REBECCA

Tax adjusted trading profit computation – year ended 31 March 2021

		£	£
Net profit			79,164
Add:	Depreciation	7,424	
	Increase in general impaired debt provision	268	
	Expenses relating to Rebecca's flat	3,000	
	Rebecca's car expenses	2,690	
	Rebecca's drawings	18,000	
	Parking fines	280	
			31,662
			110,826
Less:	Profit on sale of equipment	1,280	
	Capital allowances	11,642	
			(12,922)
Tax adjusted trading profit			97,904

Tutorial note

1   *If a sole trader makes a general provision in the accounts, it is not allowable for tax purposes, but specific provisions are allowable.*

2   *Gifts to customers costing less than £50 per person per year and carrying a conspicuous advertisement for the business are tax allowable. Therefore the cost of the diaries will be allowable.*

3   *Parking fines incurred by the owner are not allowable, even if they are incurred whilst on business activity.*

10   ARMADILLO

Tax adjusted trading profit computation – year ended 31 March 2021

		£	£
Net profit			34,890
Add:	Depreciation	2,345	
	Motor expenses (£4,788 × 50% × 50%)	1,197	
	Gift aid donation	34	
	Excess wages to wife (£19,000 – £14,500)	4,500	
			8,076
			42,966
Less:	Capital allowances		(3,460)
Tax adjusted trading profit			39,506

> **Tutorial note**
>
> 1 *50% of the motor expenses relates to Armadillo. Of that 50%, only 50% are allowable as he uses his car 50% for private purposes.*
>
> 2 *Entertaining staff is allowable for the business, irrespective of the amount spent.*
>
> 3 *The gift aid donation is not allowable in the adjustment of profits computation. Tax relief is available for the donation in Armadillo's personal income tax computation. The operation of this relief is covered in personal tax.*
>
> 4 *Salaries paid to family members are allowable provided they represent reasonable remuneration for the services provided to the business. As Armadillo's wife is paid more than the normal salary for the role she performs, the excess is not allowable.*

11 BENABI

Tax adjusted trading profit computation – year ended 31 March 2021

	£	£
Net profit		33,489
Wages and salaries – Benabi's salary	6,000	
Rent, rates and insurance	0	
Repairs to plant	0	
Advertising and entertaining – Boxes of chocolates	1,250	
Accountancy and legal costs	0	
Motor expenses – Benabi's motor expenses	1,100	
Depreciation	8,001	
Telephone and office costs	0	
Other expenses – subscription to gym	220	
	———	16,571
		———
		50,060
Capital allowances		(9,955)
		———
Adjusted net profit		40,105
		———

Tutorial note

1   Salaries paid to family members are allowable provided they represent reasonable remuneration for the services provided to the business. It is assumed that £8,000 is reasonable remuneration for Benabi's wife working in the marketing department.

2   Gifts to customers costing less than £50 per person per year and carrying a conspicuous advertisement for the business are tax allowable. However, gifts of food, drink, tobacco and vouchers are not allowable.

3   Entertaining staff is allowable for the business, irrespective of the amount spent.

4   Personal expenses, such as the subscription to the gym for the owner, are not allowable.

12   FRANKLIN LTD

	Allowable	Disallowable
Donation of £500 to Oxfam (a national charity)		✓
Donation of £100 to the local animal hospital	✓	
Advertising costs incurred in January 2020	✓	
Entertaining prospective customers in February 2020		✓
Dividends paid to shareholders on 2 January 2021		✓

Tutorial note

Donations to charity are not allowable in the adjustment of trading profits computation, with the exception of small donations to local charities.

Any donation to a national charity is not allowable in the adjustment of trading profits.

If not allowable in the adjustment of trading profits computation, relief is given as an allowable deduction from total profits in the computation of the company's taxable total profits.

Pre-trading expenditure is allowable if it is incurred in the seven years before trade commences and is expenditure that would be allowable if trade had commenced. The advertising is allowable but the entertaining would not be allowable if trade had started so is not allowable if incurred before trade starts.

Dividends are appropriations of profit and not allowable as an expense.

13 SILVAIN, ALICE, LUCILLE AND PASCAL

	Silvain	Alice	Lucille	Pascal
Should use the trading allowance	✓		✓	
Given automatically	✓			
Elect to receive			✓	
Elect not to receive		✓		
Taxable trading income (£)	0	0	2,750	3,220

Tutorial note

Silvain has trading income below £1,000, so will automatically receive the trading allowance and will have not have to declare any trading income for the tax year 2020/2021.

Alice will also automatically receive the trading allowance, but should elect to be treated on the normal basis, as she has an allowable loss, which is available for tax relief.

Lucille has trading income in excess of £1,000, so will not receive the trading allowance automatically. However, as her expenses are less than £1,000 she should elect to receive the trading allowance instead of deducting her expenses.

Pascal will also be taxed on the normal basis automatically and should not elect for a different treatment as his expenses exceed £1,000.

	Alice	Lucille	Pascal
	£	£	£
Trading income	690	3,750	6,300
Less: Expenses	(740)		(3,080)
Trading allowance		(1,000)	
	———	———	———
Trading profit / (loss to carry forward)	(50)	2,750	3,220
	———	———	———

CAPITAL ALLOWANCES

Key answer tips

In previous assessments, the biggest area of confusion has been the handling of cars. Remember that their treatment depends on the CO_2 emissions and whether they are used privately by the owner of the business – you must know the WDA available in each case and which column they should be included in. Always consider whether private use needs to be adjusted for – remember no adjustment is ever required for private use in a company, nor for the private use of an employee in a sole trader's business.

The final areas of difficulty are long periods of account for a company (which must be split into two separate periods) and the handling of capital allowances when a business ceases trading (remember no AIA, WDA or FYA should be given, simply a balancing adjustment in each column).

14   BROAD LTD

Capital allowances computation – year ended 31 December 2020

	General pool	Special rate pool	Total
	£	£	£	£
TWDV b/f		140,000	26,000	
Additions – no AIA				
Sales director's car		32,000		
Additions – with AIA				
Machinery	1,020,000			
Plant	10,000			
	———			
	1,030,000			
AIA	(1,000,000)			1,000,000
	———	30,000		
Disposals (lower of cost and SP)		(10,000)	(13,800)	
		———	———	
		192,000	12,200	
WDA (18%/6%)		(34,560)	(732)	35,292
Addition – 100% FYA				
Low emission car	34,000			
	———			
	34,000			
FYA (100%)	(34,000)			34,000
	———	Nil		
		———	———	
TWDV c/f		157,440	11,468	
		———	———	
Total allowances				1,069,292
				———

Tutorial note

1   *Private use of assets by an employee is irrelevant in a company's capital allowances computation; the allowances are available in full. The individual is assessed on the private use element in his/her personal income tax computation as an employment benefit.*

2   *Capital allowances on car purchases are calculated based on the CO_2 emissions of the car as follows:*

– *new car with CO_2 emissions of $\leq$ 50g/km:*

eligible for a FYA of 100% (i.e. Finance Director's car)

– *CO_2 emissions of between 51 – 110g/km:*

put in main pool and eligible for a WDA at 18% (i.e. Sales Director's car)

– *CO_2 emissions of > 110g/km:*

put in special rate pool – eligible for a WDA at 6%.

3   *Disposals are deducted at the lower of cost and sale proceeds. The deduction for the machinery is therefore restricted to £10,000.*

15   WELL LTD

Capital allowances computation – year ended 31 March 2021

	£	General pool £	Special rate pool £	Total £
TWDV b/f		134,500	36,000	
Additions – no AIA or FYA				
Finance Director's car		34,500		
Additions – with AIA				
Machinery	844,167			
AIA				
(£1,000,000 × 9/12) + (£200,000 × 3/12)	(800,000)			800,000
	———	44,167		
Disposals (Lower of Cost and SP)		(10,000)	(11,800)	
		———	———	
		203,167	24,200	
WDA				
18%		(36,570)		36,570
6%			(1,452)	1,452
		———	———	
TWDV c/f		166,597	22,748	
		———	———	———
Total allowances				838,022
				———

Tutorial note

1   *Private use of assets is irrelevant in a company's capital allowances computation; the allowances are available in full. The individual is assessed on the private use element in their personal income tax computation as an employment benefit.*

2   *Capital allowances on car purchases are calculated based on the CO_2 emissions of the car. As the Finance Director's new car has CO_2 emissions of between 51 – 110g/km, it is put in the main pool and is eligible for a WDA at 18%.*

The Finance Director's original car had CO_2 emissions of 145g/km and would therefore have been in the special rate pool as emissions exceed 110g/km.

3   *As the accounting period straddles 1 January 2021, the AIA must be time apportioned.*

4   *Disposals are deducted at the lower of cost and sale proceeds.*

16   PINKER LTD

(a)   **Capital allowances computation – five months ended 31 December 2020**

	General pool	Special rate pool	Total
	£	£	£	£
TWDV b/f	345,980	23,000	
Additions – no AIA or FYA			
Car	18,000		
Additions – with AIA			
Plant	539,000		
AIA (£1,000,000 × 5/12)	(416,667)		416,667
	———		
	122,333		
	486,313	23,000	
WDA (18% × 5/12)	(36,473)		36,473
WDA (6% × 5/12)		(575)	575
Addition – 100% FYA			
Low emission car	13,790		
FYA (100%)	(13,790)		13,790
	———	Nil	
TWDV c/f	449,840	22,425	
Total allowances			467,505

Tutorial note

1   *This computation is for the five month period ending 31 December 2020. Therefore you must remember to time apportion the AIA and WDAs available by 5/12, but not the FYA.*

2   *Private use of assets is irrelevant in a company's capital allowances computation. The allowances are available in full. The individual is assessed on the private use element in their personal income tax computation as an employment benefit.*

3   *Capital allowances on car purchases are calculated based on the CO_2 emissions. Cars with CO_2 emissions of between 51 – 110g/km are put in the main pool and are eligible for a WDA at 18% per annum.*

Cars with CO_2 emissions of ≤ 50g/km are eligible for a FYA of 100%.

(b)   **Short life assets**

	True	False
Short life assets have a maximum life of 6 years		✓
Annual investment allowance should be allocated against additions in the general pool before it is allocated against a short life asset	✓	
Short life assets purchased by X Ltd have a writing down allowance of 18% p.a.	✓	
It is beneficial to claim the short life asset treatment for cars		✓
Short life asset treatment is compulsory for qualifying assets		✓

Tutorial note

Short life assets can have an unlimited useful life however it may be beneficial to claim short life asset treatment where an asset has an expected life of less than eight years. A short life asset is de-pooled in the year of purchase and kept in a single asset pool column. If it has not been sold within eight years of the end of the accounting period in which it was purchased its tax written down value is transferred to the general pool at the start of the following year.

The short life asset election is not permitted for cars.

Short life asset treatment must be claimed, it is not compulsory.

17 SARAH

Capital allowances computation – year ended 31 December 2020

		General pool	Peugeot car (B.U. 80%)	Short life asset	Total
	£	£	£	£	£
TWDV b/f		65,100	14,500	7,420	
Additions – with AIA					
Furniture	11,000				
Van	8,600				
Plant	15,500				
	———				
	35,100				
AIA	(35,100)				35,100
	———	Nil			
Disposals (lower of cost and SP)		(14,200)	(10,000)	(1,400)	
		———	———	———	
		50,900	4,500	6,020	
Balancing allowance			(4,500) × 80%	(6,020)	9,620
			———	———	
WDA (18%)		(9,162)			9,162
Addition – 100% FYA					
Low emission car	20,000				
FYA (100%)	(20,000)				20,000
	———	Nil			
		———			
TWDV c/f		41,738			
		———			
Total allowances					73,882
					———

Tutorial note

1   *Private use of assets by the owner is relevant and allowances must be restricted to the business use proportion only.*

2   *Capital allowances on car purchases are calculated based on the CO_2 emissions.*

   New cars with CO_2 emissions of ≤ 50g/km are low emission cars and eligible for a FYA of 100%.

3   *CO_2 emissions are irrelevant for vans. Vans are eligible for the AIA and any balance goes into the general pool.*

4   *Short life assets may be de-pooled and when sold a balancing allowance (or charge) will arise.*

---

18 DAVE AND NICK

(a) **Capital allowances computation – eight months ended 31 August 2019**

	General pool £	Dave's car (B.U. 70%) £	Nick's car (B.U. 60%) £	Total £
	£			
Additions – no AIA or FYA				
Car		15,300	10,200	
Additions – with AIA				
Plant	7,680			
Furniture	12,450			
	20,130			
AIA	(20,130)			20,130
		Nil		
WDA (4.5%)		(689) × 70%		482
(i.e. (8% × 3/12) + (6% × 5/12))				
WDA (18% × 8/12)			(1,224) × 60%	734
TWDV c/f	Nil	14,611	8,976	
Total allowances				21,346

Tutorial note

1   *The partnership commenced on 1 January 2019 and the first accounts are prepared to 31 August 2019. This computation is therefore for an eight month period. Remember to time apportion the WDAs available by 8/12. The AIA is also time apportioned but the maximum amount of £666,667 (£1,000,000 × 8/12) exceeds the purchases in the period.*

2   *Capital allowances on car purchases are calculated based on the CO_2 emissions of the car as follows:*

   –   *new car with CO_2 emissions of ≤ 50g/km:*

         eligible for a FYA of 100% (i.e. none in this question)

   –   *CO_2 emissions of between 51 – 110g/km:*

         eligible for a WDA at 18% (i.e. Nick's car)

   –   *CO_2 emissions of > 110g/km:*

         eligible for a WDA at 8% up to 5 April 2019 then at 6% (i.e. Dave's car).

3   *Remember to calculate the allowance in full on the private use cars and then adjust for private use (i.e. only claim the business proportion of the allowance).*

(b)   **Capital allowances computation – year ended 31 August 2020**

	General pool	Dave's car (B.U. 70%)	Nick's car (B.U. 60%)	Total
	£	£	£	£
TWDV b/f	Nil	14,611	8,976	
Plant	10,000			
	————			
	10,000			
Disposal	(22,000)			
Disposal – MV		(12,500)	(7,500)	
	————	————	————	
	(12,000)	2,111	1,476	
Balancing charge	12,000			(12,000)
Balancing allowances		(2,111)	(1,476)	
	————	————	————	
		× 70%		1,478
			× 60%	886
				————
Net balancing charge				(9,636)

Tutorial note

When a business ceases to trade there is no AIA or WDA in the final accounting period. Additions are added to the relevant columns. Proceeds are compared to the TWDV of each column and balancing charges or allowances calculated.

Remember that only the business proportion of balancing allowances/balancing charges can be claimed/charged where they relate to assets with private use by an owner of the business.

19   PIRBRIGHT LTD

Capital allowances computation – year ended 30 June 2020

	General pool £	Special rate pool £	Total £
£			
TWDV b/f	81,000	28,900	
Additions – car (no AIA or FYA)		38,600	
Additions – with AIA			
Machinery	640,000		
AIA (max £1,000,000)	(640,000)		640,000
	———		
	Nil		
Disposals (lower of cost and SP)	(11,250)	(15,400)	
	———	———	
	69,750	52,100	
WDA			
18%	(12,555)		12,555
6%		(3,126)	3,126
Addition – 100% FYA			
Low emission car	21,000		
FYA (100%)	(21,000)		21,000
	———	Nil	
		———	
TWDV c/f	57,195	48,974	
	———	———	———
Total allowances			676,681
			———

Tutorial note

1   *Private use of assets is irrelevant in a company's capital allowances computation; the allowances are available in full. The individual is assessed on the private use element in his/her personal income tax computation as an employment benefit.*

2   *Capital allowances on car purchases are calculated based on the CO_2 emissions of the car. A car with CO_2 emissions in excess of 110g/km is put into the special rate pool and is eligible for a WDA.*

New cars with CO_2 emissions of ≤ 50g/km are low emission cars and eligible for a FYA of 100%.

BASIS OF ASSESSMENT

Key answer tips

When applying the basis of assessment rules be careful to start with the correct tax year, as otherwise this will have a knock on effect on the rest of your answer. You must also carefully count months, as any mistakes with this simple task will cost you marks. It is recommended that you work your answers on paper first – checking the dates and months, and ensuring that the dates seem logical. Remember that a taxpayer will always be taxed on twelve months' worth of profits, except in the first and last tax year of the business.

20 KURT

(a) C

(b) A

(c) C

(d) B

(e) £25,800

(f) B

Working

Tax year	Basis period	Assessment £
2017/18	1 October 2017 – 5 April 2018 (6/9 × £22,500)	15,000
2018/19	1 October 2017 – 30 September 2018 £22,500 + (3/12 × £43,200)	33,300
2019/20	Current year basis year ended 30 June 2019	43,200
Overlap profits	1 October 2017 – 5 April 2018 (6/9 × £22,500)	15,000
	1 July 2018 – 30 September 2018 (3/12 × £43,200)	10,800
		——
		25,800
		——

21   ROBERT

(a)   B

(b)   C

(c)   B

(d)   £17,100

Working

Tax year	Basis period	Assessment £
2018/19	1 January 2019 – 5 April 2019 (3/10 × £32,000)	9,600
2019/20	1 January 2019 – 31 December 2019 £32,000 + (2/12 × £45,000)	39,500
2020/21	Current year basis year ended 31 October 2020	45,000

Overlap profits	1 Jan 2019 – 5 Apr 2019	(3/10 × £32,000)	9,600
	1 Nov 2019 – 31 Dec 2019	(2/12 × £45,000)	7,500
			17,100

22   JAVID

Answer = C

Working

Tax year	Basis period
2019/20	1 January 2020 – 5 April 2020
2020/21	6 April 2020 – 5 April 2021

Tutorial note

The first tax year is the year in which the business commenced trading, i.e. 2019/20, therefore the second tax year is 2020/21. The opening year rules dictate that when a business does not have a year end falling inside of a tax year (2020/21) then the profits will be taxed on an actual basis (i.e. 6 April – 5 April).

23 CHARIS

Answer = B

Working

Tax year	Basis period	Assessment £
2019/20	1 January 2020 – 5 April 2020 (3/14 × £21,000)	4,500
2020/21	1 March 2020 – 28 February 2021 (12/14 × £21,000)	18,000
2021/22	Current year basis year ended 28 February 2022	24,000

Tutorial note

Where the period of account ending in the second tax year is more than 12 months then the basis period is the 12 months to the accounting date ending in the second tax year, i.e. 12 months to 28 February 2021.

24 GORDON

(a)   C

(b)   A

(c)   B

(d)   D

Working

Tax year	Basis period	Assessment £
2019/20	Penultimate year of assessment Current year basis year ended 30 June 2019	132,000
2020/21	Final period of assessment 1 July 2019 – 30 November 2020 Year ended 30 June 2020 5 months ended 30 November 2020	120,000 56,000
		176,000
	Less: Overlap profits	(22,000)
		154,000

25 HENRIETTA

(a) C

(b) C

(c) A

(d) B

(e) £4,913

(f) B

Working

Tax year	Basis period	Assessment £
2018/19	1 February 2019 – 5 April 2019 (2/16 × £7,860)	983
2019/20	6 April 2019 – 5 April 2020 (12/16 × £7,860)	5,895
2020/21	12 months ended 31 May 2020 (12/16 × £7,860)	5,895
Overlap profits	1 June 2019 – 5 April 2020 (10/16 × £7,860)	4,913

Tutorial note

There is no set of accounts ending in the second tax year, 2019/20, so the assessment is based on the profits in the tax year 6 April 2019 – 5 April 2020.

If Henrietta changes her accounting date to 31 August (I.e. later in the tax year), then the assessment for 2023/24, the year of change, will be based on 15 months of profits. Three months of existing overlap profits will be used to reduce the assessment.

26   MELISSA

(a)   D

(b)   B

(c)   A

Working

Tax year	Basis period	Assessment £
2020/21	Penultimate year of assessment Current year basis year ended 30 September 2020	12,000
2021/22	Final period of assessment 1 October 2020 – 30 June 2021	5,000
	Less: Overlap profits	(2,000)
		3,000

27   ANTONIA

(a)   B

(b)   A

(c)   D

(d)   A

Working

Tax year	Basis period	Assessment £
2019/20	Year to 31 December 2019	38,000
2020/21	12 months to the new accounting date of 30 September 2020	
	Three months to 31 December 2019 (£38,000 × 3/12)	9,500
	Nine months to 30 September 2020	46,000
		55,500

Tutorial note

Antonia must give notice of the change in the 2020/21 tax return which must be filed by 31 January 2022.

PARTNERSHIPS

Key answer tips

The allocation of assessable profits between partners is another area of difficulty that the chief assessor has highlighted in the past.

28   SUE, WILL AND TERRI

Allocation of profit

	Total £	Sue £	Will £	Terri £
Period to: A = 31 March 2020 (£84,000 × 6/12)	B = 42,000			
Allocate (3:2)		C = 25,200	D = 16,800	
Period to: E = 30 September 2020 (£84,000 × 6/12)	F = 42,000			
Allocate (2:2:1)		G = 16,800	H = 16,800	I = 8,400
	84,000	42,000	33,600	8,400

29   JENNY AND HARVEY

Allocation of profit

	Total £	Jenny £	Harvey £
Period to: 31 March 2020 (£150,000 × 3/12)	37,500		
Allocate (1:1)		18,750	18,750
Period to: 31 December 2020 (£150,000 × 9/12)	112,500		
Salary (£40,000 × 9/12)	(30,000)	30,000	
Balance allocated (1:1)	82,500	41,250	41,250
	150,000	90,000	60,000

30 SALLY, BARRY, BILL AND BEA

Allocation of profit

	Total £	Sally £	Barry £	Bill £	Bea £
Period to 31 August 2019 (3 months) Interest on capital £80,000/£100,000/£200,000/£90,000 × 5% × 3/12	5,875	1,000	1,250	2,500	1,125
Balance (4:2:2:1)	183,125	81,389	40,695	40,694	20,347
(£756,000 × 3/12)	189,000				
Period to 31 May 2020 Balance (4:3:2:2) (£756,000 × 9/12)	567,000	206,182	154,636	103,091	103,091
	756,000	288,571	196,581	146,285	124,563

31 ALVIN, SIMON AND THEODORE

Allocation of profit

	Total £	Alvin £	Simon £	Theodore £
Period to: A = 31 July 2020 (£52,800 × 6/12)	B = 26,400			
Allocate (5:3:2)		C = 13,200	D = 7,920	E = 5,280
Period to: F = 31 January 2021 (£52,800 × 6/12)	G = 26,400			
Allocate (1:1)		H = 13,200	I = 13,200	
	52,800	26,400	21,120	5,280

32 SIAN AND ELLIE

Allocation of profit

	Total £	Sian £	Ellie £	Owen £
Period to: 30 April 2020 (£36,000 × 9/12)	27,000			
Allocate (2:1)		18,000	9,000	
Period to: 31 July 2020 (£36,000 × 3/12)	9,000			
Allocate (3:2:1)		4,500	3,000	1,500
	36,000	22,500	12,000	1,500
Year ended 31 July 2021 (3:2:1)	60,000	30,000	20,000	10,000

Owen: assessable profits

2020/21

	£
Profits from 1 May 2020 to 5 April 2021 (11 months)	
Period to 31 July 2020 (3 months)	1,500
8/12 of y/e 31 July 2021 (£10,000 × 8/12)	6,667
	────
	8,167
	────

2021/22

y/e 31 July 2021	10,000
	────

Tutorial note

Partnership tax adjusted trading profits must be allocated between partners using the profit sharing arrangements of the accounting period. Once this is done the basis period rules can be applied to the profit shares of each partner to determine the taxable profits for the tax year.

Owen has just joined the partnership so opening year rules will apply to him as if he were a sole trader commencing on 1 May 2020 and preparing accounts to 31 July each year.

TRADING LOSSES

Key answer tips

The chief assessor has stated in the past that both theory and computational questions on losses seem to cause equal difficulty for learners. This is a surprise, as the expectation would be that computational questions would see a higher level of competence than theory based, but this is not the case. Learners appear to be quite confused over how losses can be relieved and show confusion over the different rules that apply to sole traders and limited companies. Since both might be seen in one task, it is very important to fully understand the rules and the connection between losses carried back, carried forward and relief in the year of the loss.

There is also evidence of learners providing incomplete answers, or simply answering a question as all true or all false, presumably as a quick guess at the answers. Unfortunately this method does not achieve good marks!

33   NICHOLAS

	True	False
A trading loss made by a company can only be offset against trading profits from the same trade when carrying the loss back		✓
A capital loss made by a company can be offset against trading profits in the year the loss is made and in future years		✓
A sole trader cannot restrict the amount of loss offset in the current year to preserve the personal allowance	✓	
A sole trader can carry forward a loss for a maximum of four years		✓

Tutorial note

1   *A company has three options for loss relief. It can offset trading losses:*

    –   *Against current year total profits only*

    –   *Against current year total profits and then carry back against total profits of the previous 12 months (i.e. cannot carry back unless the current year total profits have been relieved)*

    –   *Carry the loss forward against total profits.*

2   *Capital losses can only be set against capital gains and must be set against current year gains first. If any loss remains, it is then carried forward against future capital gains only.*

3   *A sole trader can carry forward a loss indefinitely but must agree the amount of the loss with HMRC within four years from the end of the tax year in which the loss arose.*

34   JOANNA

Answer = C

Tutorial note

A   *There is an option, but no obligation, to offset a sole trader's loss against total income in the current tax year.*

B   *A sole trader can offset trading losses against total income in the current tax year and/or prior year in any order. There is no requirement for the preceding year to be relieved first.*

C   *Correct answer.*

D   *Losses carried forward are set against trading profits only, not total income.*

35   STILTON LTD

(a)   £600

(b)   £10,200

(c)   £29,200

(d)   £Nil

(e)   A

(f)   A

Workings

Year ended 31 December	2020	2021
	£	£
Trading profit	8,000	Nil
Interest income	1,000	600
Chargeable gain	1,200	Nil
	————	————
Total profits	10,200	600
Less: Current year loss relief		(600)
Carry back 12 months	(10,200)	
	————	————
	Nil	Nil
Less: Qualifying charitable donation	(Wasted)	(Wasted)
	————	————
Taxable total profits	Nil	Nil
	————	————

Loss working

	£
Trading loss – year ended 31 December 2021	40,000
Less: Current year loss relief	(600)
Carry back relief – year ended 31 December 2020	(10,200)
Loss to carry forward	29,200

Tutorial note

The loss can be set against total profits before deducting qualifying charitable donations in the future.

36 KANE

	True	False
---	:---::	:---:
A sole trader can offset a capital loss against chargeable gains in the current and/or the previous tax year, in any order		✓
Offset of current year capital losses is restricted to leave net gains equal to the annual exempt amount		✓
A sole trader can offset a trading loss against total income in the current and/or the previous tax year, in any order	✓	
For a trading loss made by a company to be relieved in the preceding accounting period, it must first have been relieved in the current accounting period	✓	
Use of trading loss relief by a company can result in wasted qualifying charitable donations	✓	

Tutorial note

1   *Capital losses can only be set against chargeable gains and must be set against current year gains first. If any loss remains, it is then carried forward against future chargeable gains only. It is never possible to carry back capital losses.*

2   *Current year capital losses must be set against current year gains and cannot be restricted to preserve an individual's annual exempt amount (AEA). However, the offset of capital losses brought forward is after the deduction of the individual's AEA, so the AEA is not wasted.*

37   GREEN LTD

(a)   C

(b)   Nil

(c)   (£30,000 – £20,000) = £10,000

(d)   £Nil

Workings

Year ended 31 March	2021
	£
Trading profit	175,000
Interest income	30,000
Net chargeable gains (£20,000 – £20,000 capital loss b/f)	Nil
Total profits	205,000
Less: Trading loss relief b/f	(180,000)
	25,000
Less: Qualifying charitable donation	(10,000)
Taxable total profits	15,000

CORPORATION TAX COMPUTATION

38   WITHERS LTD

	Accruals basis	Paid/Receipts basis
Qualifying charitable donations		✓
Trading income	✓	
Rental income	✓	
Interest income	✓	

39   MORGAN LTD

Answer = B

Tutorial note

A long period of account must be split into two accounting periods as follows:

Accounting period 1: First 12 months

Accounting period 2: Rest of the period.

40   LONG PERIOD OF ACCOUNT

	Time apportion	Separate computation	Period in which it arises
Chargeable gains			✓
Capital allowances		✓	
Trading profits	✓		
Qualifying charitable donations			✓

41   BROUSSE

	True	False
An individual sole trader with a 15 month period ended 31 March 2021 will have a maximum AIA of £1,050,000 for capital allowance purposes	✓	
Where a car is provided to a director of a company, the director's private use of the car is not relevant when calculating capital allowances	✓	
An individual sole trader preparing a 17 month period of account must calculate two separate capital allowances computations; one for the first 12 months and the second for the balancing period		✓
A company with a nine month accounting period ending on 31 March 2021 will qualify for a 75% (100% × 9/12) first year allowance in respect of the acquisition of a new low emission car		✓
An individual sole trader with an 11 month accounting period must time apportion the available FYAs by 11/12 for capital allowance purposes		✓
The maximum AIA for a sole trader business with an eight month accounting period ending 31 December 2020 is £666,667	✓	

Tutorial note

1   The maximum AIA for a sole trader business with a 15 month accounting period ending 31 March 2021 is £1,050,000. This is calculated as £1,000,000 for the 12 month period to 31 December 2020 and £50,000 (£200,000 × 3/12) for the 3 months ending 31 March 2021.

2   The private use of assets provided by a company to its employees is ignored when calculating capital allowances.

3   A sole trader who prepares accounts for a 17 month period would prepare a single capital allowance computation for the whole period.

4   The first year allowance is not reduced where the accounting period is less than 12 months; it is always given in full.

5   First year allowances are never time apportioned.

6   The maximum AIA for a sole trader business with an eight month accounting period ending 31 December 2020 is £666,667 (£1,000,000 × 8/12).

42   TAXABLE TOTAL PROFITS

Answer = D

Tutorial note

Qualifying charitable donations are deductible on a paid basis.

Dividend income should be excluded from TTP.

Chargeable gains should be included in TTP.

Brought-forward losses are deductible against total profits before qualifying charitable donations, not TTP.

43   COUPE LTD

	Total	12 months to 30 Sept 2020	3 months to 31 Dec 2020
	£	£	£
Trading income	15,750	12,600	3,150
Capital allowances	7,000	5,000	2,000
Rental income	7,500	6,000	1,500
Interest income	3,000	2,400	600
Chargeable gain	800	800	Nil
Qualifying charitable donation	1,000	Nil	1,000

Tutorial note

Trading income is time apportioned.

Separate computations for each accounting period are required for capital allowances.

Interest income and property income are allocated on an accruals basis.

Chargeable gains are allocated according to date of disposal and qualifying charitable donations according to the date of payment.

44 MERCURY LTD

Corporation tax payable – 9 months ended 31 March 2021

	£
Trading profit	250,000
Net chargeable gains (£13,000 – £13,000 capital loss b/f)	Nil
Total profits	250,000
Less: Trading loss relief b/f	(35,000)
	215,000
Less: Qualifying charitable donation	(2,000)
Taxable total profits	213,000
Corporation tax liability at 19%	40,470

45 PANGOLIN LTD

Corporation tax payable – 16 month period ended 31 March 2021

	Year ended 30 November 2020	Four months ended 31 March 2021
	£	£
Trading profit (12:4)	60,000	20,000
Rental income (12:4)	16,500	5,500
Chargeable gain (note)	61,000	–
Total profits	137,500	25,500
Less: Qualifying charitable donation	(3,000)	–
Taxable total profits	134,500	25,500
Corporation tax liability at 19%	25,555	4,845

The total corporation tax liability is £30,400

Tutorial note

The capital loss arose in the four month period ended 31 March 2021. It cannot be deducted from the chargeable gain of the previous accounting period. It must be carried forward for relief in the future.

CHARGEABLE GAINS

EXEMPT ASSETS

46 DEBREL

	Chargeable asset	Exempt asset
Dishwasher – sold for £300		✓
Diamond bracelet – sold for £4,000 (cost £2,500)		✓
Jaguar car – sold for £70,000		✓
Exchequer stock – sold for £100,000		✓

47 BIRCH

	Chargeable asset	Exempt asset
Antique vase – sold for £23,000	✓	
Vintage classic car		✓
Unquoted shares	✓	

48 ROSE

	Chargeable asset	Exempt asset
Holiday cottage	✓	
Quoted shares in an ISA		✓
Racehorse (wasting chattel)		✓

49 LARCH

	Chargeable asset	Exempt asset
Freehold factory	✓	
Diamond necklace – sold for £17,000	✓	
Racing pigeon (wasting chattel)		✓

50 ARKWRIGHT

	Chargeable asset	Exempt asset
Quoted shares	✓	
Prize winning greyhound (wasting chattel)		✓
Painting by Monet – sold for £300,000	✓	

CHARGEABLE GAIN COMPUTATIONS

Key answer tips

The chief assessor has pointed out in the past that connected persons are an area that appears to cause problems. You may be tested both on who is connected and what the impact of that connection is and must be able to demonstrate an understanding of this.

There is also evidence that learners are struggling with indexation allowance and how to apply it accurately. In particular look out for the different presentation of some indexation information in the questions which are shown in some of the shares questions in the next section. Also consider the date to which indexation should be calculated.

51 CHARGEABLE GAIN COMPUTATIONS

		Applies to companies only	Applies to individuals only	Applies to both companies and individuals
(a)	Annual exempt amount		✓	
(b)	Indexation allowance	✓		
(c)	Rollover relief			✓
(d)	Business asset disposal relief		✓	
(e)	Investors' relief		✓	

52 WENDY

	True	False
Indexation allowance cannot create an allowable capital loss for companies	✓	
Indexation allowance can create an allowable capital loss for individuals		✓
The indexation factor is calculated to two decimal places		✓
The indexation factor is always calculated using the movement in the retail prices index from the month of expenditure to the month of disposal		✓
Indexation allowance is calculated for bonus issues in the share pool of a company		✓

Tutorial note

Indexation allowance cannot create nor increase a loss.

It is only available to companies, not individuals.

The indexation factor must be calculated to three decimal places, unless within the share pool.

Indexation will be calculated using the movement in the retail prices index from the month of expenditure to December 2017 if the asset was sold on/after that date.

Indexation is not required before recording a bonus issue, but is required before recording a rights issue.

53 SYLVESTER LTD

Allowable loss computation

	£
Deemed sale proceeds	6,000
Less: Cost	(10,000)
	(4,000)
Less: Indexation allowance	(Nil)
Allowable loss	(4,000)

Tutorial note

Where a non-wasting chattel is sold for less than £6,000, but cost more than £6,000, an allowable loss is available. However, the loss is restricted to the loss that would arise if the gross sale proceeds are deemed to be £6,000.

Indexation allowance cannot increase an allowable loss.

54 REST LTD

Answer = B

Working: Chargeable gain computation

	£
Sale proceeds	8,000
Less: Cost	(3,000)
Unindexed gain	5,000
Less: Indexation allowance (£3,000 × 0.218)	(654)
Chargeable gain	4,346
Chargeable gain cannot exceed: 5/3 × (£8,000 – £6,000)	3,333

Tutorial note

Where a non-wasting chattel is sold for more than £6,000 and it cost less than £6,000; a normal chargeable gain computation is required.

However, the gain cannot exceed the 5/3rd rule as shown above.

55 XYZ LTD

Chargeable gain computation

	£
Sale proceeds	250,000
Less: Cost	(100,000)
Extension	(22,000)
Unindexed gain	128,000
Less: Indexation allowance	
(£100,000 × 0.315)	(31,500)
(£22,000 × 0.112)	(2,464)
Chargeable gain	94,036

Tutorial note

Roof repairs are not capital and cannot be deducted in the capital gains calculation.

Improvement costs such as the extension must be indexed separately. Indexation runs from the month in which the costs were incurred.

56   LIVINGSTONE LTD

Chargeable gain computation

	£
Sale proceeds	200,000
Less: Cost £180,000 × £200,000/(£200,000 + £700,000)	(40,000)
Unindexed gain	160,000
Less: Indexation allowance (£40,000 × 0.683)	(27,320)
Chargeable gain	132,680

Tutorial note

The allowable cost in a part disposal computation is calculated using:

A/A+B   where   A = market value of the part sold

B = the market value of the remainder

Indexation runs from the month in which the costs were incurred up to December 2017 if the asset was sold on/after that date.

57   STAN

	True	False
An individual disposing of one third of an investment in land must compare one third of the original cost of the land to the sale proceeds received to calculate the chargeable gain		✓
A company is 100% owned by Mr Black. The company gifts a capital asset to Mr Black's wife. The gift will be a nil gain/nil loss disposal for capital gains purposes		✓
Stan is connected to his mother, brother, sister-in-law and niece for the purposes of capital gains tax		✓
Meera owns a painting which cost £12,000 in 2002. She gives it to a charity in 2020 when the painting is worth £50,000. She has a chargeable gain of £38,000		✓
Fred bought shares in July 2014 costing £17,500. If Fred dies in 2021 when the shares are worth £40,000, his estate will be charged capital gains tax on a gain of £22,500		✓

Tutorial note

Only gifts between husband and wife or between civil partners are made at no gain no loss. A gift from a company cannot be a no gain no loss disposal.

Stan is not connected to his niece.

Gifts to charity and disposals on death are exempt disposals.

58 TOPHAM LTD

Chargeable gain computation

	£
Sale proceeds	42,000
Less: Cost	(40,000)
	2,000
Less: Indexation allowance	
(£40,000 × 0.080) = £3,200 restricted as cannot create a loss	(2,000)
Chargeable gain	Nil

Tutorial note

Indexation allowance runs from the month in which the costs were incurred up to December 2017 if the asset was sold on/after that date, but it cannot create an allowable loss.

59 SYBILE

Chargeable gain computation

	£
Sale proceeds	160,000
Less: Cost £560,000 × £160,000/(£160,000 + £840,000)	(89,600)
	70,400
Less: Indexation allowance (not applicable for individuals)	(Nil)
Chargeable gain	70,400

60   RIZWAN

	True	False
On the disposal of a non-wasting chattel with gross sale proceeds in excess of £6,000 and cost of less than £6,000, the chargeable gain is calculated using deemed sale proceeds of £6,000		✓
Wasting chattels are exempt if disposed of by individuals or companies	✓	
On the disposal of a non-wasting chattel with gross sale proceeds in excess of £6,000 and cost of less than £6,000, the chargeable gain cannot exceed: 5/3 × (gross sale proceeds – £6,000)	✓	
On the disposal of a non-wasting chattel at a loss with gross sale proceeds and cost in excess of £6,000, the allowable loss is calculated using deemed sale proceeds of £6,000		✓

Tutorial note

The deemed sale proceeds of £6,000 are only used when a non-wasting chattel is sold at a loss; where the sale proceeds are less than £6,000 and the cost is in excess of £6,000.

Therefore, it is not applicable in the first scenario, which is a sale at a gain.

It is not applicable in the last scenario as both the cost and sale proceeds exceed £6,000. A normal allowable loss is calculated in this situation.

61   KAREN, BEN AND SARAH

(a)   **Karen**

Net chargeable gain before annual exempt amount

	£
Chargeable gains in the year (£6,000 + £7,000)	13,000
Less: Allowable capital losses in the year	(4,000)
Net chargeable gains before annual exempt amount	9,000

Tutorial note

Current year capital losses must be offset against current year gains, even if that brings the net chargeable gain below the annual exempt amount. The offset cannot be restricted to preserve the annual exempt amount.

(b) **Ben**

The correct answer is £3,400

	£
Chargeable gains in the year (£9,000 + £3,900)	12,900
Less: AEA	(12,300)
	600
Less: Allowable capital losses b/f	(600)
Taxable gains	Nil

Therefore of the £4,000 capital losses brought forward, £600 have been offset and £3,400 remain to be carried forward as at 5 April 2021

Tutorial note

Brought forward capital losses are offset after deduction of the annual exempt amount. Any unrelieved amounts continue to be carried forward to future years.

(c) **Sarah**

	£
Chargeable gains in the year (£23,000 + £7,300)	30,300
Less: Allowable capital losses in the year	(2,000)
	28,300
Less: Annual exempt amount	(12,300)
Taxable gains	16,000

	£		£
Basic rate	11,500 (£37,500 − £26,000) × 10%		1,150
Higher rate	4,500 × 20%		900
	16,000		
			2,050

DISPOSAL OF SHARES

Key answer tips

Share disposals are commonly tested. The most commonly recurring error is the handling of matching rules where shares are bought 30 days after a disposal (for individuals) or 9 days before (for companies). It is common for learners to ignore the matching rules completely and simply show one large pool that takes events in strict chronological order.

62   PUCK LTD

Chargeable gain computation

	£
Sale proceeds	24,000
Less: Cost (W)	(14,000)
Unindexed gain	10,000
Less: Indexation allowance (W) (£17,524 – £14,000)	(3,524)
Chargeable gain	6,476

Working: Share pool

	Number of shares	Cost £	Indexed cost £
June 2008	3,000	12,000	12,000
January 2012			
Bonus issue (1 for 3)	1,000	Nil	Nil
	4,000	12,000	12,000
December 2015			
Indexation update (£12,000 × 0.202)			2,424
Rights issue (1 for 4) @ £2	1,000	2,000	2,000
	5,000	14,000	16,424
December 2017			
Indexation update (£16,424 × 0.067)			1,100
	5,000	14,000	17,524
April 2020 – Disposal	(5,000)	(14,000)	(17,524)
Balance c/f	Nil	Nil	Nil

Tutorial note

Indexation is not required before recording a bonus issue, but is required before recording a rights issue and the disposal. When assets are sold on/after December 2017, indexation is only calculated up to December 2017.

Take care when reading the indexation information if it is presented in a table as in this question – you simply need to look up the row and column of the two dates and take the indexation factor from the relevant box – there is no need to do any calculations to establish the indexation factor.

63 PISTON LTD

Chargeable gain computation

	£
Sale proceeds	18,800
Less: Cost (W)	(17,770)
	————
Unindexed gain	1,030
Less: Indexation allowance (W) (£22,705 – £17,770)	
Restricted, indexation allowance cannot create a loss	(1,030)
	————
Chargeable gain	Nil
	————

Working: Share pool

	Number of shares	Cost £	Indexed cost £
August 2006	2,700	10,640	10,640
July 2013			
Bonus issue (1 for 3)	900	Nil	Nil
	————	————	————
	3,600	10,640	10,640
January 2014			
Indexation update (£10,640 × 0.268)			2,852
Acquisition	2,300	7,130	7,130
	————	————	————
	5,900	17,770	20,622
December 2017			
Indexation update (£20,622 × 0.101)			2,083
			————
			22,705
May 2020 – Disposal	(5,900)	(17,770)	(22,705)
	————	————	————
Balance c/f	Nil	Nil	Nil
	————	————	————

Tutorial note

Indexation is not required before recording a bonus issue, but is required before recording the disposal. When assets are sold on/after December 2017, indexation is only calculated up to December 2017.

Indexation allowance cannot turn a chargeable gain into a capital loss (or increase a capital loss).

64 DREAM LTD

Chargeable gain computation

	£
Sale proceeds	46,350
Less: Cost (W)	(9,333)
Unindexed gain	37,017
Less: Indexation allowance (W) (£15,409 – £9,333)	(6,076)
Chargeable gain	30,941

Working: Share pool

	Number of shares	Cost £	Indexed cost £
March 2000	6,000	12,000	12,000
June 2005			
Bonus issue (1 for 2)	3,000	Nil	Nil
	9,000	12,000	12,000
December 2017			
Indexation update (£12,000 × 0.651)			7,812
	9,000	12,000	19,812
December 2020 – Disposal	(7,000)		
(7,000/9,000) × £12,000 and £19,812		(9,333)	(15,409)
Balance c/f	2,000	2,667	4,403

Tutorial note

Indexation is not required before recording a bonus issue, but is required before recording the disposal. When assets are sold on/after December 2017, indexation is only calculated up to December 2017.

Take care when reading the indexation information if it is presented in a table as in this question – you simply need to look up the row and column of the two dates and take the indexation factor from the relevant box – there is no need to do any calculations to establish the indexation factor.

65 BATMAN LTD

Chargeable gain computation

	£
Sale proceeds (5,000 × £5)	25,000
Less: Cost (W)	(9,907)
Unindexed gain	15,093
Less: Indexation allowance (W) (£13,298 – £9,907)	(3,391)
Chargeable gain	11,702

Working: Share pool

	Number of shares	Cost £	Indexed cost £
May 2006	7,000	14,000	14,000
July 2008			
Bonus issue (1 for 8)	875	Nil	Nil
	7,875	14,000	14,000
July 2012			
Indexation update (£14,000 × 0.225)			3,150
Rights issue (1 for 5) @ £3	1,575	4,725	4,725
	9,450	18,725	21,875
December 2017			
Indexation update (£21,875 × 0.149)			3,259
	9,450	18,725	25,134
September 2020 – Disposal	(5,000)		
(5,000/9,450) × £18,725 and £25,134		(9,907)	(13,298)
Balance c/f	4,450	8,818	11,836

Tutorial note

Indexation is not required before recording a bonus issue, but is required before recording the rights issue and the disposal. When assets are sold on/after December 2017, indexation is only calculated up to December 2017.

66   SHELBYVILLE LTD

Chargeable gain computation

1   Disposal of 2,000 shares matched with the January 2021 purchase (in previous 9 days)

	£
Sale proceeds (2,000 × £3.20)	6,400
Less: Cost	(5,950)
Chargeable gain	450

2   Disposal of 3,875 shares from the pool

	£
Sale proceeds (3,875 × £3.20)	12,400
Less: Cost (W)	(8,809)
Unindexed gain	3,591
Less: Indexation allowance (W) (£9,020 – £8,809)	(211)
Chargeable gain	3,380
Total gains (£450 + £3,380)	3,830

Working: Share pool

	Number of shares	Cost £	Indexed cost £
May 2017 Purchase	10,000	23,300	23,300
November 2017 Bonus issue (1 for 40)	250	Nil	Nil
	10,250	23,300	23,300
December 2017 Indexation update (£23,300 × 0.024)			559
	10,250	23,300	23,859
February 2021 – Disposal (3,875/10,250) × £23,300 and £23,859	(3,875)	(8,809)	(9,020)
Balance c/f	6,375	14,491	14,839

Tutorial note

The matching rules for a company specify that disposals of shares are matched with:

1   *purchases on the same day, and then*

2   *purchases in the previous 9 days (FIFO basis), and then*

3   *shares held in the share pool.*

Indexation is not required before recording a bonus issue, but is required before recording the disposal. When assets are sold on/after December 2017, indexation is only calculated up to December 2017.

67 JAMES

Chargeable gain computation

	£
Sale proceeds (550 × £14.20)	7,810
Less: Cost (W)	(2,250)
Chargeable gain	5,560

Working: Share pool

	Number of shares	Cost £
July 2010	1,000	4,500
August 2012		
Bonus issue (1 for 10)	100	Nil
	1,100	4,500
October 2020 – Disposal	(550)	
(550/1,100) × £4,500		(2,250)
Balance c/f	550	2,250

Tutorial note

Indexation allowance is not given to an individual.

68 GOODWIN

Chargeable gain computation

1 Disposal of 800 shares matched with the February 2021 purchase (in next 30 days)

	£
Sale proceeds (800 × £9.00)	7,200
Less: Cost	(6,800)
Chargeable gain	400

2 Disposal of 1,700 shares from the pool

	£
Sale proceeds (1,700 × £9.00)	15,300
Less: Cost (W)	(8,925)
Chargeable gain	6,375
Total gains (£400 + £6,375)	6,775

Working: Share pool

	Number of shares	Cost £
March 2013	3,600	25,200
July 2014		
Bonus issue (1 for 3)	1,200	Nil
	4,800	25,200
January 2021 – Disposal	(1,700)	
(1,700/4,800) × £25,200		(8,925)
Balance c/f	3,100	16,275

Tutorial note

Remember to match shares sold with those acquired in the next 30 days before matching with those in the share pool.

CAPITAL GAINS – RELIEFS

Key answer tips

Historically learners have performed badly in these areas. A common question is capital losses and in particular their interaction with the annual exempt amount. An area that learners are clearly struggling with is the capital gains tax payable by individuals, using information provided regarding their taxable income. You will need to calculate the remaining basic rate band available to set against the taxable gains, before applying tax at the appropriate rates. However, take care when reading the question as it may only ask for the chargeable gain which is taxable at 10% and 20%, which means it is not necessary to actually calculate the tax itself. Also take care to identify whether the annual exempt amount has already been deducted from the figures provided or not.

69 SUSAN AND RACHEL

(a)   A

Tutorial note

Rollover relief is available where an individual or a company

- *disposes of a qualifying business asset, and*

- *replaces it with another qualifying business asset*

- *within 12 months before, and*

- *36 months after the date of disposal.*

(b)   C

Tutorial note

Business asset disposal relief is available as Susan has made a qualifying disposal and she has owned the business for at least two years.

The annual exempt amount is deducted from the antique table gain first, leaving all of the business gain to be charged to tax. The remaining gain is then taxed at 10% as business asset disposal relief is available.

The business gain must be taxed first, before the antique table gain, to use up any remaining basic rate band (if applicable).

The antique table gain, after the annual exempt amount, is therefore taxed at 20% as Susan is a higher rate taxpayer.

(c)   B

Tutorial note

Capital losses can only be set against chargeable gains, not any other income.

Current year capital losses must be set against chargeable gains of the same tax year. Any losses remaining are carried forward for offset against future chargeable gains.

(d)   D

Tutorial note

Disposals to a connected person (e.g. brother) are treated as if disposed of for their full market value at the time of the transfer.

(e)   B

Tutorial note

Shares are not a qualifying asset for rollover relief

The shares are in an unquoted trading company which have been held for at least three years. Varti does not work for the company. Therefore the conditions for investors' relief are satisfied.

Business asset disposal relief would not be available because Varti does not work for the company

The availability of investors' relief means that the gain will be taxed at 10% even though Varti is a higher rate taxpayer.

70   MALCOLM AND JEREMY

(a)   £240,000

Working: Chargeable gain computation

	£
Sale proceeds	725,000
Less: Cost	(350,000)
Chargeable gain	375,000

Chargeable at time of disposal = Lower of

(i)   Chargeable gain = £375,000

(ii)   Sale proceeds not reinvested = (£725,000 – £590,000) = £135,000

i.e. £135,000

Rollover relief is therefore the remaining gain:

(£375,000 – £135,000) = £240,000

(b)   A = 1 September 2019

         B = 1 September 2023

Tutorial note

Rollover relief is available where an individual or a company

- *disposes of a qualifying business asset, and*

- *replaces with another qualifying business asset*

- *within 12 months before, and*

- *36 months after the date of disposal.*

If all of the sale proceeds are reinvested, the whole of the chargeable gain can be deferred.

If not all of the sale proceeds are reinvested, the chargeable gain now is the lower of the

(i)   chargeable gain, or

(ii)   sale proceeds not reinvested.

The remaining gain can be deferred with a rollover relief claim.

71   AVAILABILITY OF RELIEFS

Answer = C is false

72   OLIVER LTD

Answer = C

Working

Chargeable at time of disposal = Lower of

(i)   Chargeable gain = £300,000

(ii)   Sale proceeds not reinvested = (£800,000 – £750,000) = £50,000

i.e. £50,000

Rollover relief is therefore the remaining gain:

(£300,000 – £50,000) = £250,000

Tutorial note

A   A claim must be made for rollover relief, it is not automatic.

B   Shares are not qualifying assets for the purposes of rollover relief.

C   Correct answer.

D   The time limit for reinvestment expires in May 2023; therefore a purchase in June 2023 is too late to qualify.

73   JOHN, PAUL, GEORGE AND RINGO

(a)   D

Tutorial note

A   Rollover relief is not available on disposals of shares.

B   John must work for the company for these shares to be eligible for business asset disposal relief.

C   The shares are sold for their full market value and therefore there is no gift element in the transaction.

(b)   D

Tutorial note

A   Rollover relief is only available on disposals of qualifying business assets, not vases. It is also not available on gifts.

B   Investors' relief is only available on the disposal of qualifying shares, not antique vases.

C   Gift relief is only available on the disposal of qualifying business assets, not antique vases.

(c)   C

Tutorial note

A   *Rollover relief is not available on disposals of shares.*

B   *Business asset disposal relief is only available on shares if the individual owns at least 5% of the shares and works for the company.*

C   *Gift relief is available on the sale at undervaluation of a qualifying business asset, which includes unquoted trading company shares.*

(d)   B

Tutorial note

A   *Rollover relief is not available if there is no reinvestment of sale proceeds in qualifying business assets.*

B   *Business asset disposal relief is available on the sale of a partnership interest.*

C   *The partnership interest is sold for full market value and therefore there is no gift element in the transaction.*

74   NORMAN

(a)   £68,770

Working

	£
Chargeable gain on the shares	700,000
Less: Annual exempt amount	(12,300)
Taxable gain	687,700
Capital gains tax @ 10%	68,770

Tutorial note

Business asset disposal relief will apply here which means the gain will be taxed at 10%. Norman's shareholding represents a greater than 5% interest in the company and has been working for the company. In addition, he satisfies both of these conditions for the most recent 24 months

(b)   31 January 2023

(i.e. 12 months from 31 January following the end of the tax year in which the disposal occurred)

75   HARRY AND BRIONY

(a)   D

Tutorial note

A   *Rollover relief is not available on disposals of shares.*

B   *If not all the sale proceeds are reinvested, the chargeable gain now is the **lower** of the*

    (i)   *chargeable gain, and*

    (ii)   *sale proceeds not reinvested.*

    *The **remaining gain** can be deferred with a rollover relief claim.*

C   *When rollover relief is claimed, the gain is rolled over by **deducting** the gain from the base cost of the replacement asset.*

(b)   A

Working: Capital gains tax – 2020/21

	£
Chargeable gain	5,500,000
Less: Annual exempt amount	(12,300)
Taxable gain	5,487,700
Gains qualifying for business asset disposal relief (£1,000,000 lifetime allowance – £300,000 used in 2019/20)	
= £700,000 × 10%	70,000
Remaining gain (£5,487,700 – £700,000) = £4,787,700 × 20%	957,540
	1,027,540

(c)   C

(d)   C

Tutorial note

Disposals between husband and wife are treated as 'no gain/no loss' transactions.

The market value of the asset at the date of transfer is irrelevant; the recipient spouse takes over the asset at its original cost.

The deemed disposal value of the asset is therefore the cost to the original spouse, and this is also the deemed cost for the recipient spouse.

76 CHERYL

(a)   C

(b)   C

Tutorial note

Disposals between husband and wife or civil partners are treated as 'no gain/no loss' transactions.

The market value of the asset at the date of transfer is irrelevant; the recipient takes over the asset at its original cost.

The deemed disposal value of the asset is therefore the cost to the original spouse, and this is also the deemed cost for the recipient spouse.

James makes the disposal for £120,000 and will have a gain of £70,000. He may deduct his own annual exempt amount from this gain but unused annual exempt amounts cannot be transferred between individuals.

Disposing of assets through a spouse or civil partner can be advantageous. The couple will save tax if they have unused annual exempt amount, unused basic rate band or unused capital losses to set against the gain.

(c)   A

77 ALLYN AND SIMON

(a)   £600,000

   Working: Chargeable gain computation

	£
Sale proceeds	2,850,000
Less: Cost	(1,400,000)
Chargeable gain	1,450,000

   Chargeable at time of disposal = Lower of

   (i)   Chargeable gain = £1,450,000

   (ii)   Sale proceeds not reinvested = (£2,850,000 – £2,000,000) = £850,000

   i.e. £850,000

   Rollover relief is therefore the remaining gain:

   (£1,450,000 – £850,000) = £600,000

(b)   A = 1 February 2018

   B = 1 February 2022

Tutorial note

Rollover relief is available where an individual or company

- disposes of a qualifying business asset, and

- replaces with another qualifying business asset

- within 12 months before, and

- 36 months after the date of disposal.

If all of the sale proceeds are reinvested, the whole of the chargeable gain can be deferred.

If not all of the sale proceeds are reinvested, the chargeable gain now is the lower of the

(i)   chargeable gain, and

(ii)   sale proceeds not reinvested.

The remaining gain can be deferred with a rollover relief claim.

---

78   EVAN, ZAK AND LILIA

Taxpayer	Taxable income	Chargeable gain	
		10% CGT	20% CGT
	£	£	£
Evan	21,500	16,000	92,000
Zak	29,700	7,800	100,200
Lilia	42,300	0	108,000

Tutorial note

The chargeable gains provided in the question are before the deduction of the annual exempt amount. The taxable gains in each case are therefore £108,000 (£120,300 – £12,300).

The amount of the chargeable gain taxable at 10% is calculated by deducting the taxable income from the basic rate band available of £37,500.

---

79   OPHELIA, GEORGIA AND SID

Taxpayer	Taxable income	Chargeable gain	
		10% CGT	20% CGT
	£	£	£
Ophelia	38,000	0	14,000
Georgia	24,200	13,300	700
Sid	19,850	14,000	0

Tutorial note

In this question you are provided with taxable gains after the deduction of the annual exempt amount. It is therefore not necessary to deduct the AEA – always take care when reading the question to ensure you understand the information provided.

The amount of the chargeable gain taxable at 10% is calculated by deducting the taxable income from the basic rate band available of £37,500.

NATIONAL INSURANCE CONTRIBUTIONS

SELF-EMPLOYED INDIVIDUALS

Key answer tips

Calculating the NICs payable by partners causes learners the most difficulty. Remember that it may be necessary to apportion partnership profits before calculating the class 4 NICs and that each partner will be liable to their own class 2 NICs.

80   JENNY AND JACK

(a)   **Class 4 NICs**

	£ p
(£50,000 – £9,500) = £40,500 × 9%	3,645.00
(£85,000 – £50,000) = £35,000 × 2%	700.00
	4,345.00

(b)   **Class 2 NICs**

	£ p
(£3.05 × 52 weeks)	158.60

(c)   C

Tutorial note

Self-employed taxpayers pay class 4 NICs based on their taxable trading profits in excess of £9,500 and the fixed rate class 2 NICs of £3.05 per week provided taxable trading profits exceed £6,475.

81   CARTER

Answer = C

Tutorial note

Self-employed taxpayers pay class 4 NICs based on their taxable trading profits in excess of £9,500 and the fixed rate class 2 NICs of £3.05 per week provided taxable trading profits exceed £6,475.

The taxable trading profit for the year ended 31 December 2020, which is taxed in 2020/21, is below the class 4 threshold of £9,500 but above the class 2 threshold of £6,475. Therefore there is no liability to class 4 NICs but there is a liability to class 2 NICs.

82   IVOR

(a)   **Amount liable to class 4 NICs at 9%**

(£50,000 – £9,500)   £40,500
                                                                      ─────────

(b)   **Amount liable to class 4 NICs at 2%**

(£100,000 – £50,000)   £50,000
                                                                      ─────────

(c)   **Class 2 NICs**

                                                                         £ p
(£3.05 × 52 weeks)   158.60
                                                                      ─────────

(d)   **True or false**

	True	False
Ivor will also be required to pay class 1 Primary NICs in relation to his salary from the partnership		✓

Tutorial note

Class 1 primary NICs are paid by employees. Self-employed individuals pay class 4 on their profits regardless of when those profits are drawn from the business.

83   JAKE, SUE AND PETE

(a)   **Class 2 NICs**

	£ p
(£3.05 × 52 weeks)	158.60

(b)   **Class 4 NICs**

	£ p
(£41,000 − £9,500) = £31,500 × 9%	2,835.00

(c)   £Nil

Tutorial note

Self-employed taxpayers pay class 4 NICs based on their taxable trading profits in excess of £9,500 and the fixed rate class 2 NICs of £3.05 per week provided taxable trading profits exceed £6,475.

84   THOMAS AND SUZANNE

(a)   **Amount liable to class 4 NICs at 9%**

	£ p
Thomas is past state pension age	£Nil

(b)   **Class 4 NICs**

	£ p
(£35,000 − £9,500) = £25,500 × 9%	2,295.00

(c)   D

Tutorial note

Self-employed taxpayers pay class 4 NICs based on their taxable trading profits in excess of £9,500 and the fixed rate class 2 NICs of £3.05 per week provided taxable trading profits exceed £6,475.

However, if the taxpayer has reached state pension age by the start of the tax year there is no class 4 liability.

85   AMELIE AND ALEXANDER

(a)   **Class 4 NICs payable by Amelie**

	£ p
Share of partnership profits (£75,000 – £5,000) × 60%	42,000
(£42,000 – £9,500) = £32,500 × 9%	2,925.00

(b)   **Class 4 NICs payable by Alexander**

	£ p
Share of partnership profits £5,000 + ((£75,000 – £5,000) × 40%)	33,000
(£33,000 – £9,500) = £23,500 × 9%	2,115.00

(c)   **Class 2 NICs payable by Amelie**

	£ p
(£3.05 × 52 weeks)	158.60

Tutorial note

When calculating NICs for partners you must first apportion the partnership profits between the partners following the normal partnership rules. You should then apply the normal NIC rules to those apportioned profits, not the partnership 'salary'.

Class 2 NICs are payable by all partners in full.

CURRENT TAX RELIEFS AND OTHER TAX ISSUES

R&D TAX CREDITS AND IR35

86   BARRY

	True	False
Ellis plc is an SME. It has already deducted £40,000 of qualifying research and development cost from its profits. It can deduct a further £92,000 in arriving at its adjusted trading profit.		✓
Jade plc has annual turnover below 100 million euros. It is automatically classed as an SME.		✓
The cost of heating and lighting a research and development department can never be part of the qualifying cost for R&D tax credits.		✓

87 CAITLIN

	True	False
Employers' NIC for staff involved in research and development activities can be part of the qualifying cost for R&D tax credits.	✓	
If an SME makes a loss due to qualifying research and development expenditure it must surrender the loss in return for a cash payment.		✓
Capital expenditure of £50,000 is incurred by an SME on qualifying research and development projects. The company can claim capital allowances on £115,000 (£50,000 × 230%).		✓

Tutorial note

If a loss is incurred due to R&D then it may be surrendered in return for a cash payment. It is not compulsory to do this.

Capital expenditure does not qualify for R&D tax credits.

88 JOE

	True	False
All the turnover of a personal service company (PSC) is automatically subject to a deemed employment income tax charge.		✓
IR35 legislation exists to prevent a PSC from being used to disguise permanent employment.	✓	
If a PSC has only one client it is an indication that this is a disguised employment.	✓	
If a PSC has several clients then none of its income will be subject to a deemed employment income charge.		✓

Tutorial note

A personal service company is subject to the IR35 rules where the relationship between the worker and the client would be considered to be an employment relationship if the existence of the PSC was ignored.

It is possible for a PSC to have several clients and for the IR35 rules only to apply to one or two of them. These are called relevant engagements.

In order to decide if a contract is a relevant engagement a number of factors must be considered. If a PSC only has one client then this is indicative of an employment relationship but is not conclusive on its own. Conversely if a PSC has several clients this is not a guarantee that the IR35 rules will not apply.

89   IRIS

	True	False
Central plc engages Zoom Ltd to provide some consultancy services. Zoom Ltd is a PSC. If the contract between Central plc and Zoom Ltd is deemed to be a relevant engagement under IR35 rules then Central plc must deduct income tax and NIC from the payments made to Zoom Ltd.		✓
If the owner of a PSC provides his/her own tools and equipment in carrying out a contract for a client then that contract cannot be deemed to be a relevant engagement subject to IR35 rules.		✓
If the owner of a PSC cannot send a substitute to carry out work for a client but must perform the work himself/herself, then that is an indication that the contract may be deemed to be a relevant engagement subject to IR35 rules.	✓	

Tutorial note

The client company is not subject to the IR35 rules. It is Zoom Ltd that would be subject to an employment income charge. This requires Zoom Ltd to treat the payments from Central plc as if they were a salary paid out at the end of the tax year. Zoom Ltd must deduct tax and NIC and pay employers' NIC on the deemed salary, although normal employment expenses can be deducted.

Providing own tools and equipment is an indication that the relationship is not a disguised employment but is not conclusive on its own.

A requirement to perform work personally is an indication that the relationship is a disguised employment, although it is not conclusive on its own.

SELF-ASSESSMENT

PAYMENT DATES

Key answer tips

When asked for dates it is important to state the full date, including the year, and to ensure that it is the right year! Unfortunately, if one date is wrong, they tend to all be wrong.

When calculating payments on account, you must remember which year the payments should be based on, ensure that you know what is included in the payments on account system and what is payable as part of the balancing payment. You should ensure that you state accurate dates.

90 INDIVIDUAL'S PAYMENT DATES

(a)   31 January 2021

(b)   31 January 2022

(c)   31 January 2022

(d)   31 July 2021

Tutorial note

A self-employed individual must pay 'Payments on account' for income tax and class 4 NICs, based on the previous year's income tax and class 4 NICs payable, on 31 January in the tax year and 31 July following the end of the tax year.

The final balancing payment is due on 31 January following the end of the tax year.

Capital gains tax is never paid in instalments, it is all due on 31 January following the end of the tax year.

91 PAYMENTS ON ACCOUNT (POAs)

	True	False
POAs are not required if the income tax and class 4 NIC payable for the previous year by self-assessment is less than £1,000	✓	
POAs for 2020/21 are due on 31 July 2021 and 31 January 2022		✓
POAs are not required if more than 80% of the income tax and capital gains tax liability for the previous year was met through tax deducted under PAYE		✓
POAs of class 2 NICs are never required	✓	
POAs of class 4 NICs are optional; the taxpayer can choose to pay under monthly direct debit or quarterly invoice if they prefer		✓

Tutorial note

POAs are not required if:

(i)   *the total amount of income tax and class 4 NICs payable for the previous year after the deduction of tax under PAYE is less than £1,000, or*

(ii)   *more than 80% of the income tax and class 4 NICs liability for the previous year was met through tax deducted at source.*

Capital gains tax is not taken into account when deciding whether POAs are required.

POAs are not optional. Unless the conditions above apply, POAs must be paid.

POAs are due on 31 January in the tax year (i.e. 31 January 2021) and 31 July following the end of the tax year (i.e. 31 July 2021) for 2020/21.

92 COMPANY PAYMENT DATES

     (a)   14 October 2020

     (b)   1 October 2021

     (c)   1 November 2021

     (d)   14 October 2021

Tutorial note

(a)   *The augmented profits limit of £1,500,000 is divided by two for the total number of 51% group companies (company plus one 51% group company). With a revised limit of £750,000 and augmented profits of £800,000, the company is 'large'. As it was also 'large' in the previous year it must pay its tax under the quarterly instalment rules. The first payment is due on 14th of the 7th month following the start of the accounting period.*

(b)   *With an augmented profits limit of £1,125,000 (£1,500,000 × 9/12) for the short accounting period and augmented profits of £800,000, the company is not 'large'. The due date for its tax liability is nine months and one day after the end of the accounting period.*

(c)   *With an augmented profits limit of £1,500,000 and augmented profits of £800,000, the company is not 'large'. The due date for its tax liability is nine months and one day after the end of the accounting period.*

(d)   *With an augmented profits limit of £437,500 (£1,500,000 ÷ 2 × 7/12) and augmented profits of £800,000, the company is 'large'. As it was also large in the previous year it must pay its tax under the quarterly instalment rules. The first payment is always due on 14th of the 7th month following the start of the accounting period, regardless of the length of the accounting period.*

93   DUE DATES

(a)   31 July 2021

(b)   31 October 2021

(c)   1 October 2021

(d)   Large/Current

Tutorial note

A self-employed individual must pay 'payments on account' for income tax and class 4 NICs based on the previous years' income tax payable and class 4 liability on:

(i)   31 January in the tax year, and

(ii)   31 July following the end of the tax year.

An individual can choose to file his/her return either on paper or electronically online:

(i)   If filing on paper, the due date is 31 October following the end of the tax year.

(ii)   Electronic filing must be submitted by 31 January following the end of the tax year.

The normal due date for corporation tax is nine months and one day after the end of the accounting period.

However, where the company is 'large' (i.e. its augmented profits exceed the £1,500,000 augmented profits limit), it must pay its corporation tax by quarterly instalments based on the estimated corporation tax liability for the current year.

94   COMPANY DUE DATES

(a)   31 March 2022

(b)   1 January 2022

(c)   14 October 2020

(d)   14 July 2021

Tutorial note

The normal due date for corporation tax is nine months and one day after the end of the accounting period.

However, where the company is large (i.e. has augmented profits above £1,500,000), it must pay its corporation tax by quarterly instalments.

The instalments are due on the 14th day of the 7th, 10th, 13th and 16th month after the start of the accounting period.

ADMINISTRATION, PENALTIES AND ETHICAL STANDARDS

Key answer tips

As stated before, when asked for dates it is important to state the full date, including the year, and to ensure that it is the right year! It is not possible to gain full marks here without applying the rules correctly.

Regarding penalties, it is important to be clear about which penalties apply to which offence as they all have different penalty systems – late payment and late filing in particular, but also incorrect filing and failure to keep records. The chief assessor has commented in the past that it is very common for learners to give the penalties that apply to late filing in answer to a question about late payment and vice versa. This usually results in no marks being allocated to a question on this topic.

95   IRFAN

	True	False
An individual must retain their tax records for his/her business for 2020/21 until 5 April 2023		✓
If an individual is seven months late in submitting the tax return for 2020/21, he/she will receive a maximum penalty of £200		✓
The maximum penalty for a mistake in a tax return due to carelessness is 70%		✓
If an individual's balancing payment for 2020/21 is two months late he/she can be charged a penalty for late payment of 5%	✓	
A company with a period of account ending 30 September 2020 must submit its tax return by 30 September 2021	✓	
Interest is charged on late payments of balancing payments and instalments	✓	

Tutorial note

An individual's business records must be retained for five years after the filing date (i.e. 31 January following the end of the tax year). Therefore, the 2020/21 records must be kept until 31 January 2027.

The penalties for an individual filing a tax return late are as follows:

(i)   *Within three months of the due date   =   £100 fixed penalty*

(ii) *Between three to six months of the due date = Additional daily penalties of £10 per day (Maximum 90 days)*

(iii) *Between six to 12 months of due date = Additional 5% of tax due (Minimum £300)*

(iv) *More than 12 months after the due date = Additional 5% of tax due (Minimum £300)*

(v)   *More than 12 months after the due date if the taxpayer withholds information:*

   – deliberate and concealed = 100% (Minimum £300)

   – deliberate and not concealed = 70% (Minimum £300).

The maximum penalty for incorrect returns depends on the behaviour of the taxpayer, and is calculated as a percentage of tax lost as follows:

(i)   *Mistake despite taking reasonable care – no penalty*

(ii) *Failure to take reasonable care – 30%*

(iii) *Deliberate understatement – 70%*

(iv) *Deliberate understatement with concealment – 100%.*

In addition to tax and possible interest, late payment penalties are applied to unpaid tax. However, late payment penalties only apply to the final payment of income tax, class 2 and 4 NICs and capital gains tax.

The amount due is:

(i)   *5% of the unpaid tax if it is more than one month late*

(ii) *A further 5% if more than six months late*

(iii) *A further 5% if more than 12 months late.*

A company must submit its tax return within 12 months of the end of the accounting period.

Interest is payable on any tax paid late.

96 COMPLIANCE CHECKS AND APPEALS

(a)   C

Tutorial note

HMRC must issue a written notice to initiate a compliance check and cannot issue a notice more than 12 months after the date the return was actually filed.

(b)   True or false

	True	False
A closed compliance check can be reopened within 9 months of the completion notice		✓
The taxpayer's right of appeal against an amended assessment on the closure of a compliance check must be made within 30 days of the completion notice	✓	
Where a company has submitted its tax return on time, the deadline for HMRC to commence a compliance check is two years after the end of the company's accounting period		✓
In complex tax cases HMRC can close discrete matters in a compliance check, whilst other issues remain open	✓	

Tutorial note

A closed compliance check cannot be re-opened.

Appeals must be made within 30 days.

Where a company has submitted its tax return on time, the time limit for commencing a compliance check is one year after the actual filing date.

HMRC can issue a Partial Closure Notice to close discrete matters in a complex compliance check.

(c)   A

Tutorial note

An appeal can only be made on the basis of a point of law.

Note that the Supreme Court was previously known as the House of Lords.

97   NAGINA

	True	False
The maximum penalty for failing to keep records is £3,000 per accounting period	✓	
The maximum penalty for a failure to notify chargeability is 100% of the tax due but unpaid	✓	
A late payment penalty can apply to payments on account of income tax		✓
Companies can choose whether to file paper tax returns or file online		✓

Tutorial note

The maximum penalty for notifying chargeability depends on the behaviour of the taxpayer, and is calculated in broadly the same way as the penalty for an incorrect return.

The late payment penalty only applies to the final payments of income tax and class 4 NICs and to the payment of class 2 NICs and capital gains tax, not payments on account.

Companies must file their returns online.

98   PENALTIES

(a)   B

(b)   C

(c)   A

(d)   A

Tutorial note

Penalties for submitting a company's or an individual's tax return late are as follows:

(i)   Within three months of the due date = £100 fixed penalty

(ii)   Between three to six months of the due date = £200 fixed penalty

(iii)   Between six to 12 months of due date = Additional 10% of tax due

(iv)   More than 12 months after the due date = Additional 20% of tax due

> The maximum penalty for incorrect returns depends on the behaviour of the taxpayer, and is calculated as a percentage of tax lost as follows:
>
> (i)   Mistake despite taking reasonable care – no penalty
>
> (ii)   Failure to take reasonable care – 30%
>
> (iii) Deliberate understatement – 70%
>
> (iv)   Deliberate understatement with concealment – 100%.

99   MANINDER

	True	False
The filing deadline for electronic submission of an individual's 2020/21 tax return is 31 January 2022	✓	
A self-employed individual is required to keep records to support his/her 2020/21 tax return until 31 January 2027	✓	
There is no penalty for late submission of an individual's tax return as long as it is less than six months late		✓
If a company makes a mistake in the tax return due to failure to take reasonable care, there is a penalty of up to 30%	✓	
An individual should make the first payment on account for 2020/21 on 31 January 2022		✓

Tutorial note

An individual can choose to file the tax return either on paper or electronically online:

(i)   If filing on paper, the due date is 31 October following the end of the tax year.

(ii)   Electronic filing must be submitted by 31 January following the end of the tax year.

An individual's business records must be retained for five years after the filing date (i.e. 31 January following the end of the tax year). Therefore, the 2020/21 records must be kept until 31 January 2027.

Penalties for submitting an individual's tax return late are as follows:

(i)   Within three months of the due date   =   £100 fixed penalty

(ii)   Between three to six months of the due date   =   Additional daily penalties of £10 per day (Maximum 90 days)

(iii) Between six to 12 months of due date   =   Additional 5% of tax due (Minimum £300)

(iv)   More than 12 months after the due date   =   Additional 5% of tax due (Minimum £300)

(v)   More than 12 months after the due date if the taxpayer withholds information:

– deliberate and concealed = 100% (Minimum £300)

– deliberate and not concealed = 70% (Minimum £300).

The maximum penalty for a company making a mistake on their return depends on the behaviour of the company, and is calculated as a percentage of tax lost as follows:

(i)   Mistake despite taking reasonable care – no penalty

(ii)   Failure to take reasonable care – 30%

(iii)   Deliberate understatement – 70%

(iv)   Deliberate understatement with concealment – 100%.

A self-employed individual must pay 'Payments on account' for income tax and class 4 NICs based on the previous year's results on:

(i)   31 January in the tax year, and

(ii)   31 July following the end of the tax year.

100   JANET

	True	False
If an individual is eight months late in submitting the tax return for 2020/21, he/she will receive a penalty of £200		✓
The maximum penalties for errors made by individuals in their tax returns vary from 20% to 100%		✓
If a company fails to keep records for the appropriate period of time, it can be fined up to £2,000		✓
A company with a period of account ending on 30 June 2020, must keep its records until 30 June 2028		✓
Late payment penalties are not normally imposed on payments on account	✓	

Tutorial note

Penalties for submitting an individual's tax return late are as follows:

(i)   *Within three months of the due date   =   £100 fixed penalty*

(ii)   *Between three to six months of the due date   =   Additional daily penalties of £10 per day (Maximum 90 days)*

(iii)   *Between six to 12 months of due date   =   Additional 5% of tax due (Minimum £300)*

(iv)   *More than 12 months after the due date   =   Additional 5% of tax due (Minimum £300)*

(v)   *More than 12 months after the due date if the taxpayer withholds information:*

    – deliberate and concealed = 100% (Minimum £300)

    – deliberate and not concealed = 70% (Minimum £300).

> The maximum penalty for errors made by an individual in his/her tax return depends on the behaviour of the taxpayer, and is calculated as a percentage of tax lost as follows:
>
> (i)   Mistake despite taking reasonable care – no penalty
>
> (ii)   Failure to take reasonable care – 30%
>
> (iii)   Deliberate understatement – 70%
>
> (iv)   Deliberate understatement with concealment – 100%.
>
> Companies must keep records until six years from the end of the accounting period.
>
> The maximum penalty for a company failing to keep records is £3,000 per accounting period affected.
>
> Late payment penalties only apply to the final payment of income tax, class 2 and 4 NICs and capital gains tax, not payments on account.

101   ETHICAL RULES (1)

Key answer tips

Make sure you read written questions like this very carefully.

In part (a) the question is asking you which statement is NOT correct; it is very easy to misread and ignore the not.

(a)   The answer is C.

The other three statements are correct.

Tutorial note

Whilst an accountant can be associated with returns that may omit information which would mislead HMRC, this is only true provided the information was not deliberately omitted and is more in the nature of supplementary information which would enhance understanding.

An accountant should not be associated with a return which has deliberately omitted sources of income or other information about taxable income.

(b)   The answer is C.

Tutorial note

The accountant can only share information with the client, unless the client gives authority for others to be informed.

102 ETHICAL RULES (2)

(a) The answer is D.

The other three statements are correct.

Tutorial note

It is common practice for accountants to prepare tax returns for clients. However, the accountant can only prepare the return based on the information supplied by the client.

The client must always sign the return and the declaration included on the return, to confirm that he/she has supplied all relevant information.

It is the client's responsibility to submit a completed, signed form as his/her self-assessment of his/her own tax position.

(b) The answer is C.

Tutorial note

An accountant generally needs the client's permission before revealing confidential information.

103 CLIENT ADVICE

(a) The answer is C.

The other three statements are correct.

Tutorial note

Tax evasion (such as deliberately failing to disclose all of your income) is illegal.
It is tax avoidance that uses legal means to reduce your tax bill.

(b) The answer is C.

104 AAT STUDENT

(a) The answer is B.

The other three statements are correct.

Tutorial note

The duty of confidentiality to the client applies in all circumstances to all individuals, except where there is a legal, regulatory or professional duty to disclose (e.g. suspicion of money laundering).

An accountant cannot therefore disclose information to anyone without the client's permission, including the client's spouse or civil partner.

(b)   The answer is D.

Tutorial note

When money laundering is suspected an accountant should report his/her suspicions. This legal duty overrules the duty of confidentiality.

105 NASHEEN

	True	False
If a husband is ill, it is acceptable to discuss his tax affairs with his wife even if no letter of authorisation exists.		✓
Accountants must follow the rules of confidentiality irrespective of the situation.		✓

Tutorial note

The first statement is false because the duty of confidentiality to the client applies in all circumstances to all individuals, except where there is a legal, regulatory or professional duty to disclose (e.g. suspicion of money laundering).

An accountant cannot therefore disclose information to anyone without the client's permission, including the client's spouse or civil partner.

The second statement is false because when money laundering is suspected an accountant should report his/her suspicions. This legal duty overrules the duty of confidentiality.

106 TAX RETURN RESPONSIBILITY

The answer is C.

A taxpayer is ultimately responsible for ensuring that his/her tax return is accurately completed.

107   LAREDO

	True	False
All tax records for an individual should be kept for at least four years.		✓
The maximum penalty for not keeping records is £2,000.		✓
An individual whose income tax and class 4 NIC payable by self-assessment for the previous tax year is less than £1,000 is not required to make payments on account.	✓	
Tax on chargeable gains is paid in two instalments on 31 January in the tax year and 31 July following the end of the tax year.		✓

Tutorial note

Tax records should be kept for one year from 31 January following the tax year for personal records and five years for business records.

Taxpayers can be fined up to £3,000 for failure to keep records.

There are no instalments for capital gains tax.

The whole of the capital gains tax liability is due on 31 January following the end of the tax year (i.e. 31 January 2022 for the 2020/21 tax year).

WRITTEN QUESTIONS

Key answer tips

To answer a written question, you must make sure you have understood the scenario you are being asked about, and that your answer is specific to that situation and not just generalised facts. The chief assessor comments that often learners give very generic, basic answers that may be technically correct, but are not directly related to the scenario given.

108 MALIK

Dear Malik

Congratulations on the new contract. The new contract means that you will be required to pay both class 4 and class 2 national insurance contributions.

Class 2 national insurance contributions are currently at a fixed rate of £3.05 per week and therefore you would pay £3.05 × 52 = £158.60 per year, based on current figures.

Class 4 contributions are based on 9% of your taxable profits above the current limit of £9,500. Once you have estimated figures, I can provide more detailed calculations. If you are making payments on account of income tax, the class 4 contributions are paid in the same way. However, as your income tax payable was less than £1,000 for 2020/21, you do not have to make payments on account of income tax or national insurance for 2021/22. We will need to revisit this issue for 2022/23.

If you have any further queries please contact me.

AAT student

109 BAMBOO LTD

With regard to the understated rent, this appears to be a genuine mistake, rather than the financial controller not taking appropriate care. Your financial controller immediately informed HMRC of the issue. As a result, there should be no penalty.

The corporation tax return for Elm Ltd for the year ended 30 June 2019 was due by 30 June 2020. As the return was filed on 7 June 2020, it was not late and no penalty will be incurred.

If you have any further queries please contact me.

AAT student

Tutorial note

The maximum penalty for errors made in the tax return depends on the behaviour of the taxpayer, and is calculated as a percentage of tax lost as follows:

(i)   *Mistake despite taking reasonable care – no penalty*

(ii)   *Failure to take reasonable care – 30%*

(iii)   *Deliberate understatement – 70%*

(iv)   *Deliberate understatement with concealment – 100%.*

110 SARA

Dear Sara

In response to your query, HMRC have the right to enquire into your 2019/20 tax return. They can start a compliance check within 12 months of the date that your return was filed, so they are within their powers, as you filed your return six months ago.

You should only send documents and written particulars to HMRC if they are requested as a part of the compliance check process.

If the check is complex and there are multiple matters, it is possible that HMRC will issue a Partial Closure Notice after one or more matters are resolved, whilst leaving other issues open.

At the end of the compliance check, a completion notice will be issued to you with details of the outcome. You have the right to appeal this notice within 30 days, via an informal review or a formal appeal to the Tax Tribunal, which is an independent body.

Please let me know if you need further assistance with this.

AAT student

Tutorial note

HMRC must issue a written notice to initiate a compliance check and cannot issue a notice more than 12 months after the date the return was actually filed.

111 CHARLIE

Dear Charlie,

Payments on account of your tax liability for any year must be paid by 31 January in that tax year, and by 31 July following the end of the tax year. This is based on an estimate, using the preceding tax years' tax payable.

Therefore, when you made your tax payments on 31 January 2021 and 31 July 2021 for 2020/21, this was based on your tax payable for 2019/20.

When the final figures are sent to HMRC, if these two payments on account are not enough to cover the full liability, a balancing payment is due on the 31 January following the tax year.

For 2020/21 your payments due will therefore be:

31 January 2021	(£8,600/2)	£4,300
31 July 2021	(£8,600/2)	£4,300
31 January 2022	(£9,000 – £8,600)	£400

I hope this makes things clearer. If you have any queries please do not hesitate to contact me.

Best regards

AAT Student

Tutorial note

A self-employed individual must pay 'Payments on account' for income tax and class 4 NICs based on the previous years' results on:

(i)   31 January in the tax year, and

(ii)   31 July following the end of the tax year.

112 MELANIE

Whether Melanie will be treated as carrying on a trade

An item of furniture could be a trading asset or an investment or for personal use so the 'nature of asset' test is inconclusive.

The work carried out by Melanie in restoring the furniture would indicate that the furniture is a trading asset.

Melanie's motive in purchasing more furniture to renovate and sell is partly to make a profit, which is indicative of trading.

It is unlikely that the items of furniture **inherited** by Melanie will be regarded as trading assets. However, additional items of furniture **purchased** by Melanie for renovation and sale are likely to be regarded as trading assets.

Melanie is an investment banker. Restoring and selling furniture is not similar to any trading activity carried on by Melanie.

(Note: you were only required to explain Melanie's position in relation to four factors.)

113 CHARLOTTE

Charlotte,

Here is the information you requested. I hope it is helpful.

Tax payments

Income tax is paid by two instalments (known as payments on account), the first on the 31 January in the tax year (31 January 2021 for 2020/21) and the second on the 31 July after the tax year (31 July 2021 for 2020/21).

These are based on half of your prior year income tax payable. No payments on account are made for capital gains tax.

Due on 31 January 2022

On 31 January 2022 you will have to pay the balance of any income tax due for 2020/21 and all of your 2020/21 capital gains tax. In your case this will be £6,230 which is your total liability of £14,230 less the £8,000 you have already paid by payments on account.

In addition you will have to pay the first payment on account for your 2021/22 income tax. This will be £4,665 as it is based on half of your 2020/21 income tax payable of £9,330.

This means that you must pay a total of £10,895 by 31 January 2022.

Consequences of late payment

If you pay tax late, then you are charged interest from the date you should have paid until the day the tax is actually paid.

In addition, if you make your balancing payment of £6,230 late you may be charged a late payment penalty. If the payment is more than 30 days late a penalty of 5% of the tax due can be charged which increases if the tax is paid more than six months late.

Kind regards

AAT student

Tutorial note

In addition to tax and possible interest, late payment penalties are applied to unpaid tax. However, late payment penalties only apply to the final payment of income tax, class 4 NICs and capital gains tax.

The amount due is:

(i)   5% of the unpaid tax if it is more than 30 days late

(ii)   A further 5% if more than six months late

(iii)   A further 5% if more than 12 months late.

114   SOPHIA

There are several issues involved with not disclosing income to HMRC. Luckily this has not been going on for a long time so the consequences are not as bad as they could be.

1   Altering your 2019/20 tax return

Amendments to a tax return can be made by a taxpayer up to 12 months after the filing date. For a 2019/20 return the filing date was 31 January 2021. You can therefore make an amendment to your return to include the interest income and this should be done by 31 January 2022.

2   Penalty for incorrect return

As you have omitted some income from your tax return you have made an incorrect return. A penalty may be charged by HMRC and this varies according to whether they consider it to be a careless or deliberate error. A careless error can attract a penalty of up to 30% of the tax unpaid as a result of the error and a deliberate error a maximum penalty of 70% of unpaid tax.

The tax unpaid as a result of your error is £ 600 (40% of £1,500).

The penalties can be reduced if you disclose the income voluntarily before HMRC become aware of it. In your case it is likely that HMRC will treat this as a careless error and the maximum penalty they will charge is £180 (£600 × 30%) although this may be reduced down to nil due to your disclosure.

3   Late payment penalty and interest

As well as a penalty for an incorrect return, interest will be due on the unpaid tax from the date it should have been paid (i.e. 31 January 2021).

A late payment penalty can also be charged. As the tax is between six and 12 months late this penalty could be 10% of the outstanding tax.

Best regards

AAT Student

Tutorial note

If the taxpayer files an incorrect tax return, a penalty equal to a percentage of the tax under declared may be charged. The penalty may be waived for inadvertent errors, as long as the taxpayer notifies HMRC of the error as soon as possible.

The percentage depends on the reason for the error.

Taxpayer behaviour	Maximum penalty (% of tax lost)
Mistake despite taking reasonable care	*No penalty*
Failure to take reasonable care	*30%*
Deliberate understatement	*70%*
Deliberate understatement with concealment	*100%*

The penalties may be reduced at HMRC discretion, depending on the type of penalty and whether the taxpayer makes an unprompted disclosure of the error.

TAX RETURNS

Key answer tips

The chief assessor has highlighted the most common errors made by learners in this task in the past.

In the self-employed return there are two main errors made by learners. One is to forget to adjust for the depreciation shown in the first column. The same figure should always appear in both box 29 and 44. Also, some learners simply list the disallowed figures in the first boxes in the second (disallowable expenses) column, in any order. So if there are five adjustments to be made, boxes 32 to 36 would be completed. It is important to note the narrative for each box and to include the disallowable items in the appropriate box to match the equivalent expense entry in the left hand column.

115 JORDAN

Business expenses
Please read the 'Self-employment (full) notes' before filling in this section.

	Total expenses	Disallowable expenses	
	If your annual turnover was below £85,000, you may just put your total expenses in box 31	Use this column if the figures in boxes 17 to 30 include disallowable amounts	
17	Cost of goods bought for resale or goods used	£ 208178 . 00	32 £ . 00
18	Construction industry – payments to subcontractors	£ . 00	33 £ . 00
19	Wages, salaries and other staff costs	£ 35604 . 00	34 £ 18000 . 00
20	Car, van and travel expenses	£ 13112 . 00	35 £ 2690 . 00
21	Rent, rates, power and insurance costs	£ 14240 . 00	36 £ 3000 . 00
22	Repairs and maintenance of property and equipment	£ 340 . 00	37 £ . 00
23	Phone, fax, stationery and other office costs	£ 742 . 00	38 £ . 00
24	Advertising and business entertainment costs	£ . 00	39 £ . 00
25	Interest on bank and other loans	£ . 00	40 £ . 00
26	Bank, credit card and other financial charges	£ . 00	41 £ . 00
27	Irrecoverable debts written off	£ 1540 . 00	42 £ 268 . 00
28	Accountancy, legal and other professional fees	£ 980 . 00	43 £ . 00
29	Depreciation and loss/profit on sale of assets	£ 6144 . 00	44 £ 6144 . 00
30	Other business expenses	£ 1778 . 00	45 £ 280 . 00
31	Total expenses (total of boxes 17 to 30)	£ 282658 . 00	46 Total disallowable expenses (total of boxes 32 to 45) £ 30382 . 00

Adapted from SA103F 2020, page 2, HMRC

116   BINTOU

Business expenses

Please read the 'Self-employment (full) notes' before filling in this section.

Total expenses	Disallowable expenses
If your annual turnover was below £85,000, you may just put your total expenses in box 31	Use this column if the figures in boxes 17 to 30 include disallowable amounts

	Total expenses		Disallowable expenses
17	Cost of goods bought for resale or goods used £ 1 0 8 1 9 5 · 0 0	32	£ · 0 0
18	Construction industry – payments to subcontractors £ · 0 0	33	£ · 0 0
19	Wages, salaries and other staff costs £ 6 5 6 5 0 · 0 0	34	£ 3 0 0 0 · 0 0
20	Car, van and travel expenses £ 1 0 1 1 0 · 0 0	35	£ 1 4 4 0 · 0 0
21	Rent, rates, power and insurance costs £ 1 2 2 5 0 · 0 0	36	£ 4 0 0 0 · 0 0
22	Repairs and maintenance of property and equipment £ · 0 0	37	£ · 0 0
23	Phone, fax, stationery and other office costs £ 2 7 5 5 · 0 0	38	£ · 0 0
24	Advertising and business entertainment costs £ 8 6 6 5 · 0 0	39	£ 2 3 1 0 · 0 0
25	Interest on bank and other loans £ · 0 0	40	£ · 0 0
26	Bank, credit card and other financial charges £ · 0 0	41	£ · 0 0
27	Irrecoverable debts written off £ 5 1 0 · 0 0	42	£ · 0 0
28	Accountancy, legal and other professional fees £ 2 9 8 0 · 0 0	43	£ · 0 0
29	Depreciation and loss/profit on sale of assets £ 1 6 1 4 0 · 0 0	44	£ 1 6 1 4 0 · 0 0
30	Other business expenses £ 1 7 6 0 · 0 0	45	£ · 0 0
31	Total expenses (total of boxes 17 to 30) £ 2 2 9 0 1 5 · 0 0	46	Total disallowable expenses (total of boxes 32 to 45) £ 2 6 8 9 0 · 0 0

Adapted from SA103F 2020, page 2, HMRC

117   LYNNE AND SHIRLEY PETERS

Partnership Statement (short) for the year ended 5 April 2021

Please read these instructions before completing the Statement

Use these pages to allocate partnership income if the only income for the relevant
return period was trading and professional income or untaxed interest and alternative
finance receipts from UK banks and building societies. Otherwise you must download the
'Partnership Statement (Full)' pages to record details of the allocation of all the partnership
income. Go to www.gov.uk/taxreturnforms

Step 1   Fill in boxes 1 to 29 and boxes A and B as appropriate. Get the figures you need
from the relevant boxes in the Partnership Tax Return. Complete a separate
Statement for each accounting period covered by this Partnership Tax Return and
for each trade or profession carried on by the partnership.

Step 2   Then allocate the amounts in boxes 11 to 29 attributable to each partner using the
allocation columns on this page and page 7, read the Partnership Tax Return
Guide, go to www.gov.uk/taxreturnforms
If the partnership has more than 3 partners, please photocopy page 7.

Step 3   Each partner will need a copy of their allocation of income to fill in their personal
tax return.

PARTNERSHIP INFORMATION
If the partnership business includes a trade or
profession, enter here the accounting period for
which appropriate items in this statement
are returned.

Start   **1** | 01 /04 /20

End   **2** | 31 /03 /21

Nature of trade   **3** | Event organisers

MIXED PARTNERSHIPS

Tick here if this Statement is drawn up using Corporation Tax rules **4** [ ]   Tick here if this Statement is drawn up using tax rules for non-residents **5** [ ]

Individual partner details

6 Name of partner   Lynne Peters
Address

Postcode

Date appointed as a partner
(if during 2019–20 or 2020–21) Partner's Unique Taxpayer Reference (UTR)

7 | / /   **8**

Date ceased to be a partner
(if during 2019–20 or 2020–21) Partner's National Insurance number

9 | / /   **10**

Partnership's profits, losses, income and tax credits	Tick this box if the items entered in the box had foreign tax taken off	**Partner's share of profits, losses, income and tax credits** Copy figures in boxes 11 to 29 to boxes in the individual's Partnership (short) pages as shown below	
• for an accounting period ended in 2020-21 ▼			
from box 3.83 Profit from a trade or profession **A**	**11** £ 230,400	Profit **11** £ 138,240	Copy this figure to box 8
from box 3.82 Adjustment on change of basis	**11A** £	**11A** £	Copy this figure to box 10
from box 3.84 Loss from a trade or profession **B**	**12** £	Loss **12** £	Copy this figure to box 8
from box 3.94 Disguised remuneration	**12A**	**12A**	Copy to box 15
• for the period 6 April 2020 to 5 April 2021*			
from box 7.9A Income from untaxed UK savings	**13** £ 6,210	**13** £ 3,726	Copy this figure to box 28
from box 3.97 CIS deductions made by contractors on account of tax	**24** £	**24** £	Copy this figure to box 30
from box 3.98 Other tax taken off trading income	**24A** £	**24A** £	Copy this figure to box 31
from box 3.117 Partnership charges	**29** £	**29** £	Copy this figure to box 4, 'Other tax reliefs' section on page Ai 2 in your personal tax return

* If you're a 'CT Partnership' see the Partnership Tax Return Guide

Adapted from SA800 2020, HMRC

Section 3

MOCK ASSESSMENT QUESTIONS

TASK 1 (12 marks)

Safari Ltd, a UK company, has the following statement of profit or loss for the year ended 30 June 2020:

	£	£
Revenue		350,569
Less: Cost of sales		(195,053)
Gross profit		155,516
Other income		10,000
Wages and salaries	29,009	
Rent and rates	10,272	
Loss on the sale of a machine	400	
Repairs and maintenance	3,516	
Travelling and entertaining	2,357	
Motor expenses	2,814	
Legal and professional fees	4,123	
Irrecoverable debts	(756)	
Depreciation	3,656	
Other general expenses	1,225	
		(56,616)
Net profit		108,900

The following further information is given:

1 **Other income**

This comprises bank deposit interest of £7,000 for the year received on 30 June 2020, and rent receivable of £3,000 for the year ended 30 June 2020.

2 **Repairs and maintenance**

Included in this item is £1,740 incurred for replacing an obsolete machine with a new state-of-the-art version and £300 for the redecoration of a new office.

3 **Travelling and entertaining expenses**

These include expenses of entertaining UK customers of £391 and gifts to customers of bottles of champagne costing £634 (cost approximately £45 each).

4   **Legal and professional fees**

The figure in the accounts is made up as follows:

	£
Legal fees in connection with new office purchase	390
Legal fees in connection with action by customer regarding faulty goods	996
Payment to customer for breach of contract	1,440
Accountancy charges	1,297

5   **Irrecoverable debts**

The figure in the accounts is made up as follows:

	£
Trade debt recoveries	(278)
Decrease in provision for irrecoverable debts	(478)
	(756)

6   **Other general expenses**

These include a donation of £240 to the Labour Party, and a donation of £30 to the NSPCC (a national charity).

Use the grid below to calculate the adjusted trading profit of the year for tax purposes. Where you wish to deduct a figure put it in brackets. If an item needs no adjustment include a zero '0'.

	£
Net profit	108,900
Bank deposit interest	
Rent receivable	
Wages and salaries	
Rent and rates	
Loss on the sale of a machine	
Replacing obsolete machine	
Redecoration of new office	
Entertaining UK customers	
Gifts to customers	
Motor expenses	
Legal fees in connection with new office purchase	
Legal fees in connection with action by customer regarding faulty goods	
Payment to customer for breach of contract	
Accountancy charges	
Trade debt recoveries	
Decrease in provision for irrecoverable debts	
Depreciation	
Labour Party donation	
NSPCC donation	
Tax adjusted trading profit	

TASK 2 (14 marks)

Scharrett Ltd has the following non-current asset information for the seven month period ended 31 July 2020:

	£
Balances brought forward as at 1 January 2020:	
General pool	14,000
Special rate pool	16,000
Additions in January 2020:	
Machinery	590,250
Finance Director's Car (Nissan) (40% private use)	15,000
Managing Director's Car (Audi) (75% private use)	32,000
Disposals in February 2020:	
Machinery (Cost £11,000)	10,100
Managing Director's car (Renault) (Cost £17,200)	13,600

The cars have CO_2 emissions as follows:

Nissan	48g/km
Audi	106g/km
Renault	185g/km

Use the grid below to calculate Scharrett Ltd's total capital allowances and show the balances to carry forward to the next accounting period.

TASK 3 (12 marks)

(a) Kenza started trading on 1 January 2017. She prepared her first set of accounts to 31 May 2018 and then to 31 May each year.

The adjusted profits were as follows:

	£
Period ended 31 May 2018	19,040
Year ended 31 May 2019	43,200
Year ended 31 May 2020	48,000

(i) In which tax year did Kenza start trading?

  A   2015/16

  B   2016/17

  C   2017/18

  D   2018/19

(ii) What are Kenza's taxable trading profits for the first tax year of trading?

  A   £19,040

  B   £4,760

  C   £4,480

  D   £3,360

(iii) What are Kenza's taxable trading profits for the second tax year of trading?

  A   £43,200

  B   £19,040

  C   £13,440

  D   £15,680

(iv) What are Kenza's taxable trading profits for the third tax year of trading?

  A   £13,440

  B   £19,040

  C   £38,240

  D   £43,200

(v) What are Kenza's taxable trading profits for the fourth tax year of trading?

  A   £13,440

  B   £43,200

  C   £47,200

  D   £48,000

(vi) What are Kenza's overlap profits?   £ ☐

(b)   Gavin and Stacey are in partnership, and have always shared profits in the ratio 60%:40%.

It was then decided that from 1 June 2020 Gavin would be awarded a salary of £24,000 per annum to recognise the extra work that he had taken on. The remainder of the profits continue to be shared in the ratio 60%:40%.

For the year ended 31 January 2021, the tax adjusted trading profits were £180,000.

Calculate the 2020/21 assessment for each partner.

Gavin	£
Stacey	£

TASK 4   (12 marks)

(a)   Mark the following statements as true or false

	True	False
If a company pays interest on a loan to buy a new factory, the interest is deducted from non-trade interest income in the corporation tax computation.		
Legal costs incurred in writing off an irrecoverable debt due from a customer may be deducted from non-trade interest income in the corporation tax computation.		
Augmented profits includes all dividends received during the accounting period.		
Small donations to local charities must be disallowed in arriving at trading profits and relieved as qualifying charitable donations.		
The accrued amount of qualifying charitable donations is deducted from total profits to arrive at taxable total profits.		
If Ennis Ltd (an SME) spends £80,000 on qualifying research and development it can deduct a total of £184,000 in arriving at its adjusted trading profit.		

(b)   Walkden Ltd has previously prepared accounts to 31 December. In 2020 the company changes its year end and prepares accounts from 1 January 2020 to 31 May 2021.

The adjusted trading profit for the period before deducting capital allowances is £690,540.

At 1 January 2020 there was a balance in the general pool of £90,000. Plant and machinery costing £185,000 was purchased on 1 September 2020.

Complete the following grid:

	First period	Second period
Period ends on: (Insert date)		
Length of period (Insert number of months)		
Adjusted trade profits before CAs	£	£
Capital allowances	£	£
Adjusted trade profit after CAs	£	£

(c)   Due dates

   (i)   What is the deadline for the payment of corporation tax for a single company with the year end 31 August 2020 that has augmented profits below £1,500,000?

   [   ]

   (ii)   By when must a company with the year ended 31 May 2020 submit its corporation tax return?

   [   ]

   (iii)   What is the last instalment payment date for a large company with a 31 March 2021 year end?

   [   ]

TASK 5 (4 marks)

(a)   Matthew's sole trader business has made an accounting profit of £5,500 for 2020/21. His tax adjusted trading profit was £6,600

   The total amount of NICs payable by Matthew (to the nearest pence) is: £ [   ]

(b)   Ting has taxable trading profits of £53,000 for 2020/21.

   The total amount of class 4 NICs payable by Ting (to the nearest pence) is: £ [   ]

(c)   Jackie's business has made a taxable trading profit of £80,000 for 2020/21.

   The amount of class 2 NICs payable by Jackie for the year (to the nearest pence) is: £ [   ]

TASK 6 (6 marks)

(a)   For each of the following types of loss for a company, tick which income it can be set against in the **current year**:

   Note that if a loss can be set against total profits you should only tick that column.

	Trading profits	Chargeable gains	Property income	Total profits before QCDs	No loss relief available
Trading loss					
Capital loss					

(b)   For each of the following types of loss for a company, tick which income it can be set against in the **prior year**:

   Note that if a loss can be set against total profits you should only tick that column.

	Trading profits	Chargeable gains	Property income	Total profits before QCDs	No loss relief available
Trading loss					
Capital loss					

(c)   For each of the following types of loss for a company, tick which income it can be set against in the **following year**:

Note that if a loss can be set against total profits you should only tick that column.

	Trading profits	Chargeable gains	Property income	Total profits before QCDs	No loss relief available
Trading loss					
Capital loss					

TASK 7   (10 marks)

(a)   You recently received the following email from Liam, a self-employed individual, who is one of your clients.

> Due to a recent flood at our premises, we are moving to a small temporary office next week. My accounts assistant, Jenny, has recommended that, for the sake of confidentiality, I shred all of the business tax records that relate to 2018/19 (the tax year in which I started my business) as I have not had any queries regarding my income tax returns and all are finalised. Obviously I'll keep my personal records at home. I presume that is OK.
>
> Jenny has also recommended that I delay my next income tax balancing payment for two months, just to help with cash flow following the flood. I presume that is acceptable?
>
> Can you reply to me about these two issues, please?

Prepare an appropriate response to Liam.

(b)   Dominic asks whether the following statements are true or false.

Tick the appropriate box for each statement.

	True	False
The maximum penalty for mistakes in a tax return due to carelessness is 50%		
A company with a period of account ending 30 September 2020 must pay a penalty of £3,000 if it does not retain its records until 30 September 2026		
Interest is charged on late payment of balancing payments only, not payments on account		
If an individual's balancing payment for 2020/21 is two months late, a late payment penalty of 5% can be charged		
If an individual is eight months late in submitting the tax return for 2020/21, he/she will receive a penalty of £200		
Only AAT members, not students, are governed by the AAT ethical code		
There are no circumstances in which client confidentiality can be breached		

TASK 8 (6 marks)

Complete the return below for the partnership as a whole and for Mary Wall using the following information.

Mary and Fred Wall have traded in partnership for many years as bakers, sharing profits 4:3, however, from 1 October 2020 they changed the profit sharing arrangement to 1:1.

Their tax adjusted trading profits for the year ended 31 January 2021 are £189,588.

Partnership Statement (short) for the year ended 5 April 2021

Please read these instructions before completing the Statement

Use these pages to allocate partnership income if the only income for the relevant return period was trading and professional income or untaxed interest and alternative finance receipts from UK banks and building societies. Otherwise you must download the 'Partnership Statement (Full)' pages to record details of the allocation of all the partnership income. Go to www.gov.uk/taxreturnforms

Step 1   Fill in boxes 1 to 29 and boxes A and B as appropriate. Get the figures you need from the relevant boxes in the Partnership Tax Return. Complete a separate Statement for each accounting period covered by this Partnership Tax Return and for each trade or profession carried on by the partnership.

Step 2   Then allocate the amounts in boxes 11 to 29 attributable to each partner using the allocation columns on this page and page 7, read the Partnership Tax Return Guide, go to www.gov.uk/taxreturnforms
If the partnership has more than 3 partners, please photocopy page 7.

Step 3   Each partner will need a copy of their allocation of income to fill in their personal tax return.

PARTNERSHIP INFORMATION

If the partnership business includes a trade or profession, enter here the accounting period for which appropriate items in this statement are returned.

Start **1** / /

End **2** / /

Nature of trade **3**

MIXED PARTNERSHIPS

Tick here if this Statement is drawn up using Corporation Tax rules **4**

Tick here if this Statement is drawn up using tax rules for non-residents **5**

Individual partner details

6 Name of partner

Address

Postcode

Date appointed as a partner
(if during 2019–20 or 2020–21) Partner's Unique Taxpayer Reference (UTR)

7 / / **8**

Date ceased to be a partner
(if during 2019–20 or 2020–21) Partner's National Insurance number

9 / / **10**

Partnership's profits, losses, income and tax credits

Tick this box if the items entered in the box had foreign tax taken off ▼

Partner's share of profits, losses, income and tax credits

Copy figures in boxes 11 to 29 to boxes in the individual's Partnership (short) pages as shown below

● for an accounting period ended in 2020-21

from box 3.83	Profit from a trade or profession **A**	**11** £	Profit **11** £	Copy this figure to box 8
from box 3.82	Adjustment on change of basis	**11A** £	**11A** £	Copy this figure to box 10
from box 3.84	Loss from a trade or profession **B**	**12** £	Loss **12** £	Copy this figure to box 8
from box 3.94	Disguised remuneration	**12A**	**12A**	Copy to box 15

● for the period 6 April 2020 to 5 April 2021*

from box 7.9A	Income from untaxed UK savings	**13** £	**13** £	Copy this figure to box 28
from box 3.97	CIS deductions made by contractors on account of tax	**24** £	**24** £	Copy this figure to box 30
from box 3.98	Other tax taken off trading income	**24A** £	**24A** £	Copy this figure to box 31
from box 3.117	Partnership charges	**29** £	**29** £	Copy this figure to box 4, 'Other tax reliefs' section on page Ai 2 in your personal tax return

* If you're a 'CT Partnership' see the Partnership Tax Return Guide

Adapted from SA800 2020, HMRC

TASK 9 (8 marks)

(a) Lena disposed of five assets in 2020/21.

Tick the appropriate box to indicate which disposals are chargeable assets and which are exempt assets for capital gains tax purposes.

	Chargeable asset	Exempt asset
Antique sideboard – sold for £23,000 to an auction house		
Vintage classic car – Morris Minor worth £55,000 – gifted to daughter		
Unquoted shares in Febroy Ltd – sold for less than they were bought for		
Treasury stock quoted on the UK stock exchange – sold on the open market for considerably more than it was bought for		
Holiday home in Wales – sold at a profit to neighbours. Lena lives in her main residence in Birmingham		

(b) Pelican Ltd sold an antique vase for £8,450 in August 2020.

It was purchased in May 2010 for £3,180.

The relevant indexation factor is 0.244.

Which of the following is the correct chargeable gain?

A £4,494

B £5,270

C £Nil – it is an exempt asset

D £4,083

(c) Vincent Ltd owns 20 hectares of land, which it bought in May 2000 for £168,000.

In August 2020, Vincent Ltd sold eight hectares for £235,000, when the remaining 12 hectares had a market value of £320,000.

The indexation factor from May 2000 to December 2017 was 0.629.

The indexation factor from May 2000 to August 2020 was 0.735.

Complete the following computation:

£

Sale proceeds

Cost

Indexation allowance

Chargeable gain

TASK 10 (10 marks)

Pageant plc bought 1,500 shares in Calcot Ltd for £14,500 on 15 July 2012.

A bonus issue of 1 for 6 shares was made on 7 May 2013.

On 31 October 2020 the company bought 400 shares for £15.50 per share.

On 5 November 2020, the company sold 750 shares for £16.80 per share.

Indexation factors were:

July 2012 to May 2013	0.033
May 2013 to December 2017	0.112
July 2012 to December 2017	0.149
May 2013 to November 2020	0.194
July 2012 to November 2020	0.233
October 2020 to November 2020	0.003

Calculate the chargeable gain on the disposal of these shares.

TASK 11 (6 marks)

(a)   A factory was sold by Olivia for £950,000 in October 2020 realising a gain of £370,000.

Which of the following statements is correct in relation to rollover relief?

A   If Olivia purchases a replacement factory for £900,000 in June 2021 then she can use rollover relief to defer £320,000 of the gain

B   If Olivia purchases a replacement factory for £980,000 in November 2023 then she can use rollover relief to defer all the gain

C   If Olivia purchases some shares in an unquoted trading company for £980,000 in February 2021 then she can claim rollover relief

D   If Olivia reinvests in a qualifying asset within the qualifying time period then the gain of £370,000 is automatically deferred

(b)   Elvis has disposed of several capital assets in 2020/21 and realised the following gains and losses:

	Disposal to:	£
Chargeable gain	Aunt	23,300
Chargeable gain	Unconnected person	14,500
Allowable loss	Brother	(3,000)
Allowable loss	Friend	(2,600)

Elvis has unutilised capital losses relating to 2019/20 of £5,600.

(i)   What is Elvis's taxable gain for 2020/21?   £

(ii)   What is the capital loss remaining to carry forward to 2021/22?   £

(c)   Tony has taxable income of £33,215 for 2020/21. He has made a gain on the disposal of a painting of £26,300. The basic rate band for 2020/21 is £37,500.

(i)   What is Tony's capital gains tax liability for 2020/21?   £

(ii)   What is the due date of payment?

Section 4

MOCK ASSESSMENT ANSWERS

TASK 1

Safari Ltd – Adjusted trading profit – year ended 30 June 2020

	£
Net profit	108,900
Bank deposit interest	(7,000)
Rent receivable	(3,000)
Wages and salaries	0
Rent and rates	0
Loss on the sale of a machine	400
Replacing obsolete machine	1,740
Redecoration of new office	0
Entertaining UK customers	391
Gifts to customers	634
Motor expenses	0
Legal fees in connection with new office purchase	390
Legal fees in connection with action by customer regarding faulty goods	0
Payment to customer for breach of contract	0
Accountancy charges	0
Trade debt recoveries	0
Decrease in provision for irrecoverable debts	0
Depreciation	3,656
Labour Party donation	240
NSPCC donation	30
Tax adjusted trading profit	106,381

Tutorial note

1   *Depreciation, the loss on the sale of the machine, the cost of the new machine and legal fees in relation to the new office are all capital in nature and must be added back.*

2   *The £300 redecoration costs in respect of the new office are considered to be allowable revenue expenditure.*

3   *Entertaining is not an allowable deduction, unless it is in respect of entertaining staff.*

4   *Gifts to customers costing less than £50 per person per year and carrying a conspicuous advertisement for the business are tax allowable, unless they are gifts of food, drink, tobacco or vouchers. Although the bottles of champagne cost less than £50 each, the cost is disallowed as the gift is of drink.*

> 5   Legal fees and payment in connection with faulty goods are allowable, as they are trade related costs.
>
> 6   Donations to political parties are not allowable deductions.
>
> 7   Donations to a national charity are not allowable trading expenses, regardless of size.
>
> Such donations made by a company are allowable for tax, but not as a deduction in the adjustment of profits computation. They must therefore be added back and relief is given as a deduction from total profits in the TTP computation.

TASK 2

Scharrett Ltd – Capital allowances computation – seven months ended 31 July 2020

		General pool	Special rate pool	Total
	£	£	£	£
TWDV b/f		14,000	16,000	
Additions – No AIA				
Managing director's car (Audi)		32,000		
Additions – With AIA				
Machinery	590,250			
AIA (W)	(583,333)			583,333
	———	6,917		
Disposals (Lower of Cost and SP)		(10,100)	(13,600)	
		———	———	
		42,817	2,400	
WDA				
(18% × 7/12)		(4,496)		4,496
(6% × 7/12)			(84)	84
Addition – 100% FYA				
Low emission car (Nissan)	15,000			
FYA (100%)	(15,000)			15,000
	———	Nil		
		———	———	
TWDV c/f		38,321	2,316	
		———	———	
Total allowances				602,913
				———

Working: The maximum AIA for the seven months ended 31 July 2020 is £583,333 (£1,000,000 × 7/12).

Tutorial note

1   *Private use of assets by an employee is irrelevant in a capital allowances computation; the allowances are available in full. The individual is assessed on the private use element in his/her personal income tax computation as an employment benefit.*

2   *Capital allowances on car purchases are calculated based on the CO_2 emissions of the car as follows:*

–   *new car with CO_2 emissions of ≤ 50g/km:*

eligible for a FYA of 100% (i.e. the Nissan)

–   *CO_2 emissions of between 51 – 110g/km:*

put in main pool and eligible for a WDA at 18% (i.e. the Audi)

–   *CO_2 emissions of > 110g/km:*

put in special rate pool (i.e. the Renault) and eligible for a WDA at 8% up to 31 March 2019, then 6% thereafter.

3   *Disposals are deducted at the lower of cost and sale proceeds. The deduction for the machinery is therefore £10,100.*

4   *The accounting period is seven months in length, therefore the AIA and the WDA must be time apportioned by 7/12. However, the FYA is never time apportioned.*

TASK 3

Kenza

(a)   (i)   B

(ii)   D

(iii)   C

(iv)   A

(v)   B

(vi)   £11,200

Working

Tax year	Basis period		Assessment £
2016/17	Actual basis		
	1 January 2017 – 5 April 2017	(3/17 × £19,040)	3,360
2017/18	Actual basis		
	6 April 2017 – 5 April 2018	(12/17 × £19,040)	13,440
2018/19	12 months ending 31 May 2018		
	1 June 2017 – 31 May 2018	(12/17 × £19,040)	13,440
2019/20	Current year basis		
	year ended 31 May 2019		43,200
Overlap profits	1 June 2017 – 5 April 2018	(10/17 × £19,040)	11,200

(b)   **Allocation of profits**

	Total	Gavin	Stacey
	£	£	£
Period to: 31 May 2020 (£180,000 × 4/12)	60,000		
	———		
Allocate (60%:40%)		36,000	24,000
Period to: 31 January 2021 (£180,000 × 8/12)	120,000		
Salary (£24,000 × 8/12)	(16,000)	16,000	
	———		
Balance allocated (60%:40%)	104,000	62,400	41,600
	———	———	———
	180,000	114,400	65,600
	———	———	———

TASK 4

Walkden Ltd

(a)   Mark the following statements as true or false

	True	False
If a company pays interest on a loan to buy a new factory, the interest is deducted from non-trade interest income in the corporation tax computation.		✓
Legal costs incurred in writing off an irrecoverable debt due from a customer may be deducted from non-trade interest income in the corporation tax computation.		✓
Augmented profits includes all dividends received during the accounting period.		✓
Small donations to local charities must be disallowed in arriving at trading profits and relieved as qualifying charitable donations.		✓
The accrued amount of qualifying charitable donations is deducted from total profits to arrive at taxable total profits.		✓
If Ennis Ltd (an SME), spends £80,000 on qualifying research and development it can deduct a total of £184,000 in arriving at its adjusted trading profit.	✓	

Tutorial note

1   Interest on a loan to buy a new factory is trade interest and can be deducted from trade profits.

2   Costs of writing off an irrecoverable debt due from a customer relate to a trade debt and are normal trading expenses. The cost of writing off a **loan** to a customer would be a non-trade item, but that is not the case here.

3   Augmented profits excludes dividends from 51% group companies.

4   Small donations to local charities are allowed as trade expenses not as QCDs.

5   QCDs are allowed on a paid basis, not an accrued basis.

6   Companies which are small or medium sized enterprises (SMEs), can deduct a total of 230% of the cost of qualifying research and development from their profits.

     If Ennis Ltd spends £80,000 it can deduct a total of £184,000 (£80,000 × 230%) in arriving at its adjusted trade profits.

(b)

	First period	**Second period**
Period ends on: (Insert date)	31 December 2020	31 May 2021
Length of period (Insert number of months)	12	5
Adjusted trade profits before CAs	£487,440	£203,100
Capital allowances	£201,200	£5,535
Adjusted trade profit after CAs	£286,240	£197,565

Workings

(1)   Adjusted trade profits before CAs

	£	£
Adjusted trade profits split 12/17 : 5/17	487,440	203,100

(2)   **Walkden Ltd – Capital allowances computation**

	£	General pool £	Total allowances £
12 months to 31 December 2020			
Balance b/f		90,000	
Addition qualifying for AIA	185,000		
Less: AIA (max £1,000,000)	(185,000)		185,000
	———	Nil	
WDA (£90,000 × 18%)		(16,200)	16,200
		———	
Tax WDV c/f		73,800	———
Total allowances			201,200
			———
5 months to 31 May 2021			
WDA (£73,800 × 18% × 5/12)		(5,535)	5,535
		———	
Tax WDV c/f		68,265	
		———	
			5,535
			———

Tutorial note

When a company prepares accounts for a period exceeding 12 months it will have two accounting periods, the first for 12 months and the second for the balance of the period.

The adjusted trading profit before capital allowances must be time apportioned into the two periods.

Two separate capital allowances computations must be prepared, one for each period. The second period will be less than 12 months so any AIA or WDA must be time apportioned.

(c)   **Due dates**

(i)   1 June 2021
(i.e. nine months and one day after the end of the accounting period)

(ii)   31 May 2021
(i.e. 12 months after the end of the financial accounting period)

(iii)   14 July 2021
(i.e. 14th day of the 16th month after the start of the accounting period)

TASK 5

Matthew, Ting and Jackie

(a)   £158.60 (£3.05 × 52 weeks). Class 2 NICs are due where taxable trading profits exceed £6,475.

(b)   Class 4 NICs

	£ p
(£50,000 − £9,500) = £40,500 × 9%	3,645.00
(£53,000 − £50,000) = £3,000 × 2%	60.00
	————
	3,705.00
	————

(c)   Class 2 NICs

	£ p
(£3.05 × 52 weeks)	158.60
	————

Tutorial note

Self-employed taxpayers pay class 4 NICs based on their taxable trading profits in excess of £9,500 and the fixed rate class 2 NICs of £3.05 per week provided taxable trading profits exceed £6,475.

TASK 6

Losses

(a)   Income the company can set its loss against in the **current year**

	Trading profits	Chargeable gains	Property income	Total profits before QCDs	No loss relief available
Trading loss				✓	
Capital loss		✓			

(b)   Income the company can set its loss against in the **previous year**

	Trading profits	Chargeable gains	Property income	Total profits before QCDs	No loss relief available
Trading loss				✓	
Capital loss					✓

(c)   Income the company can set its loss against in the **following year**

	Trading profits	Chargeable gains	Property income	Total profits before QCDs	No loss relief available
Trading loss				✓	
Capital loss		✓			

TASK 7

(a)   **Reply to query**

> Dear Liam
>
> With regard to your business records, you are required to keep them for five years from the filing date for each return. For example, your records for 2018/19 should be kept until 31 January 2025 (i.e. five years from the normal filing date of 31 January 2020). I would therefore advise you to retain your business tax records as failure to so do can lead to a penalty of up to £3,000.
>
> Should you wish to delay your next balancing payment by two months, you will incur interest and penalties. Interest on the amount not paid will be payable from the due date until the date of payment. In addition, if you delay your balancing payment by more than 30 days you will also incur a penalty, as well as interest. The penalty is calculated as 5% of the amount of tax overdue.
>
> Please contact me again if you require further advice.

(b)   **Dominic**

	True	False
The maximum penalty for mistakes in a tax return due to carelessness is 50%		✓
A company with a period of account ending 30 September 2020 must pay a penalty of up to £3,000 if it does not retain its records until 30 September 2026	✓	
Interest is charged on late payment of balancing payments only, not payments on account		✓
If an individual's balancing payment for 2020/21 is two months late, a late payment penalty of 5% of tax due can be charged	✓	
If an individual is eight months late in submitting the tax return for 2020/21, he/she will receive a penalty of £200		✓

	True	False
Only AAT members not students are governed by the AAT ethical code		✓
There are no circumstances in which client confidentiality can be breached		✓

Tutorial note

The maximum penalty for incorrect returns depends on the behaviour of the taxpayer, and is calculated as a percentage of tax lost as follows:

(i)   Mistake despite taking reasonable care – no penalty

(ii)   Failure to take reasonable care – 30%

(iii)   Deliberate understatement – 70%

(iv)   Deliberate understatement with concealment – 100%.

A company must retain its records for six years after the end of the accounting period. The maximum penalty for not retaining records is up to £3,000.

Late payment interest is charged on **all** late payments of tax at a daily rate from the due date to the date of payment.

It is the late payment penalty that is only levied on balancing payments (of income tax, class 2 and 4 NICs and capital gains tax) and not payments on account.

The amount due is:

(i)   5% of the unpaid tax if it is more than one month late

(ii)   A further 5% if more than six months late

(iii)   A further 5% if more than 12 months late.

Penalties for submitting an individual's tax return late are as follows:

(i)   Within three months of the due date = £100 fixed penalty

(ii)   Between three to six months of the due date = Additional daily penalties of £10 per day (Maximum 90 days)

(iii)   Between six to 12 months of due date = Additional 5% of tax due (Minimum £300)

(iv)   More than 12 months after the due date = Additional 5% of tax due (Minimum £300)

(v)   More than 12 months after the due date if the taxpayer withholds information:

– deliberate and concealed = 100% (Minimum £300)

– deliberate and not concealed = 70% (Minimum £300).

The duty of confidentiality can be breached for legal or regulatory reasons (e.g. money laundering).

TASK 8

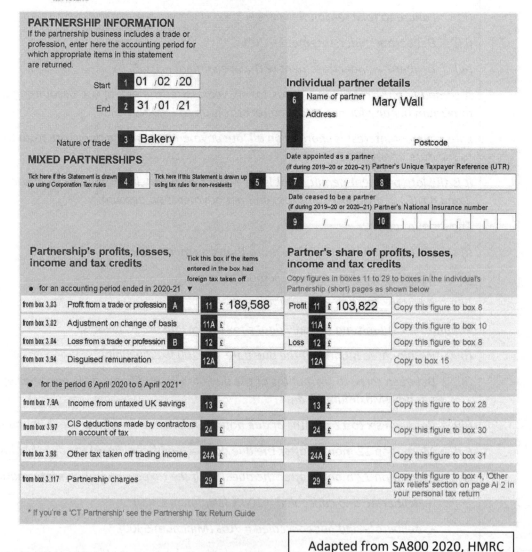

Working: Allocation of profit

	Total £	Mary £	Fred £
Period to: 30 September 2020 (£189,588 × 8/12)	126,392		
Allocate (4:3)		72,224	54,168
Period to: 31 January 2021 (£189,588 × 4/12)	63,196		
Allocate (1:1)		31,598	31,598
	189,588	103,822	85,766

TASK 9

(a) **Lena**

	Chargeable asset	Exempt asset
Antique sideboard – sold for £23,000 to an auction house	✓	
Vintage classic car – Morris Minor worth £55,000 – gifted to daughter		✓
Unquoted shares in Febroy Ltd – sold for less than they were bought for	✓	
Treasury stock quoted on the UK stock exchange – sold on the open market for considerably more than it was bought for		✓
Holiday home in Wales – sold at a profit to neighbours. Lena lives in her main residence in Birmingham	✓	

Tutorial note

The sideboard is a chattel (i.e. tangible moveable property), but it is not exempt from capital gains tax as it was not purchased and sold for less than £6,000.

Cars are exempt assets, whether sold or gifted is not relevant; there is no chargeable gain or allowable loss arising on the disposal.

Unquoted shares are chargeable assets, whether they are sold for a gain or loss is not relevant.

Treasury stock is exempt from capital gains tax, whether a capital profit or loss is made on the disposal is not relevant.

An individual's principal private residence is exempt from capital gains tax, but not a second holiday home.

(b)   Answer = D

Working: Chargeable gain computation

	£
Sale proceeds	8,450
Less: Cost	(3,180)
	5,270
Less: Indexation allowance (£3,180 × 0.244)	(776)
Chargeable gain	4,494
Chargeable gain cannot exceed:	
5/3 × (£8,450 – £6,000)	4,083

Tutorial note

Where a non-wasting chattel is sold for more than £6,000 and it cost less than £6,000; a normal chargeable gain computation is required.

However, the gain cannot exceed the 5/3rd rule as shown above.

(c)   **Vincent Ltd – Chargeable gain computation**

	£
Sale proceeds	235,000
Less: Cost £168,000 × (£235,000/(£235,000 + £320,000))	(71,135)
Less: Indexation allowance (£71,135 × 0.629)	(44,744)
Chargeable gain	119,121

Tutorial note

Indexation for companies is not available after 31 December 2017, therefore the indexation factor up to December 2017 must be used, not the factor to the month of disposal.

TASK 10

Chargeable gain computation

	£

Sale of 400 shares matched with purchase in previous nine days

	£
Sale proceeds (400 × £16.80)	6,720
Cost (400 × £15.50)	(6,200)
Unindexed gain	520
Less: Indexation allowance (N/A)	0
Chargeable gain	520

Sale of 350 shares from the pool

	£
Sale proceeds (350 × £16.80)	5,880
Less: Cost (W)	(2,900)
Unindexed gain	2,980
Less: Indexation allowance (W) (£3,332 – £2,900)	(432)
Chargeable gain	2,548
Total gain (£520 + £2,548)	3,068

Working: Share pool

	Number of shares	Cost £	Indexed cost £
July 2012	1,500	14,500	14,500
May 2013			
Bonus issue (1 for 6)	250	Nil	Nil
	1,750	14,500	14,500
Indexed rise July 2012 to Dec 2017			
0.149 × £14,500			2,161
	1,750	14,500	16,661
November 2020			
Disposal	(350)		
(350/1,750) × £14,500/£16,661		(2,900)	(3,332)
Balance c/f	1,400	11,600	13,329

Tutorial note

The matching rules for a company specify that disposals of shares are matched with:

1   purchases on the same day, and then

2   purchases in the previous nine days (FIFO basis), and then

3   shares held in the share pool.

Indexation allowance is not required before recording a bonus issue, but is required before recording the disposal.

Indexation is not available after 31 December 2017.

TASK 11

(a)   Answer = A

Working:

Chargeable at time of disposal = Lower of

(i)   Chargeable gain = £370,000

(ii)   Sale proceeds not reinvested = (£950,000 – £900,000) = £50,000

i.e. £50,000

Rollover relief is therefore the remaining gain:

(£370,000 – £50,000) = £320,000

Tutorial note

A   Correct answer.

B   The time limit for reinvestment expires in October 2023; therefore a purchase in November 2023 is too late to qualify.

C   Qualifying assets for rollover relief purposes do not include shares.

D   A claim must be made for rollover relief; it is not automatic.

(b)   (i)   **Taxable gain**

		£
Chargeable gains (£23,300 + £14,500)		37,800
Less: Current year allowable losses (Note)		(2,600)
		35,200
Less: Annual exempt amount		(12,300)
		22,900
Less: Capital losses brought forward		(5,600)
Taxable gain		17,300

(ii)   **Capital loss left to carry forward**

	£
Loss on disposal to brother (Note)	3,000

Tutorial note

The loss arising on the disposal to the brother is a connected person loss.

It cannot be set against other gains. It can only be carried forward and set against gains arising from disposals to the same brother in the future.

(c)   (i)   **Capital gains tax liability**

		£
Capital gains		26,300
Less: Annual exempt amount		(12,300)
Taxable gains		14,000

£		£
4,285 (W)	× 10%	429
9,715	× 20%	1,943
14,000		2,372

Working

	£
Basic rate band	37,500
Less: Taxable income	(33,215)
Basic rate band unused	4,285

Tutorial note

Capital gains are taxed at 10% if they fall below the basic rate threshold and 20% if they fall above the threshold.

(ii)   Due date of payment is 31 January 2022